Creating
and
Implementing
Your
Strategic Plan

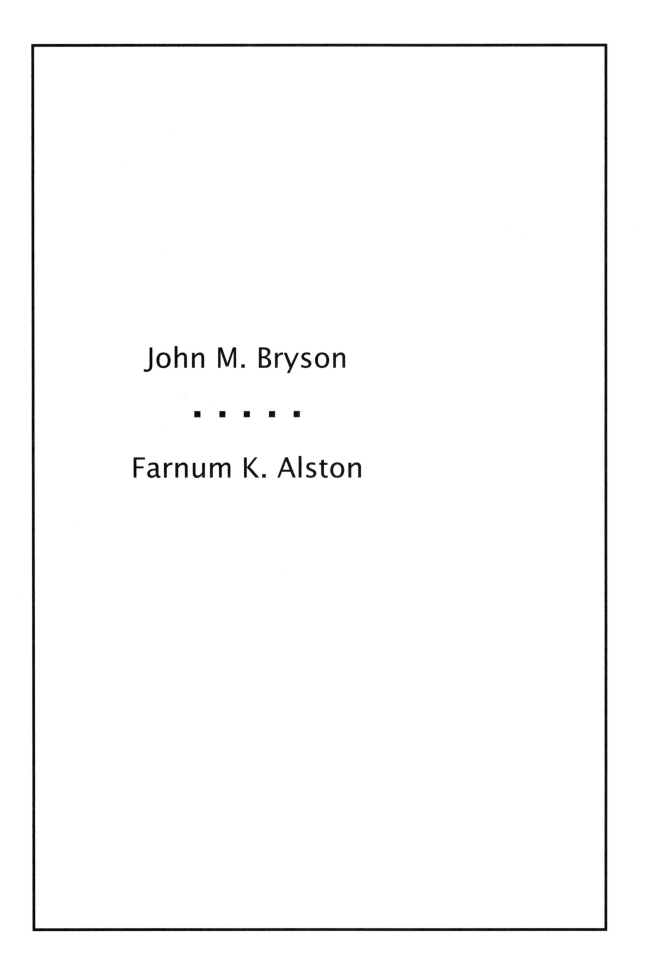

John M. Bryson

. . . . .

Farnum K. Alston

Creating
and
Implementing
Your
Strategic Plan

. . . . .

A **Workbook** for **Public** and **Nonprofit** **Organizations**

SECOND EDITION

JOSSEY-BASS
A Wiley Imprint
www.josseybass.com

Published by Jossey-Bass
A Wiley Imprint
989 Market Street, San Francisco, CA 94103-1741   www.josseybass.com

Jossey-Bass books and products are available through most bookstores. To contact Jossey-Bass directly, call our Customer Care Department within the U.S. at 800-956-7739, outside the U.S. at 317-572-3986, or fax 317-572-4002.

Jossey-Bass also publishes its books in a variety of electronic formats. Some content that appears in print may not be available in electronic books.

ISBN: 0-7879-6754-8

Printed in the United States of America
SECOND EDITION
PB Printing   10 9 8 7 6 5 4 3

Contents

Preface to the Second Edition

Strategic planning has become a way of life for the majority of public and nonprofit organizations since the publication of the first edition of this workbook in 1996 as a companion to the second edition of *Strategic Planning for Public and Nonprofit Organizations* (Bryson, 1995). We are pleased to have played a role in bringing about that change through our publications and through the more than 400 major strategic planning processes we have helped facilitate.

The basic approach we outlined in the first edition has proven as valid today as when we first proposed it. However, the field has changed as the world of theory and practice has evolved. This second edition embodies much of what we have learned since publication of the first edition.

Why has strategic planning become standard practice for most public and nonprofit organizations? The reasons are all too familiar as public and nonprofit organizations and communities face a bewildering array of challenges, including the following:

- Changing and significantly increased—or reduced—demands for their programs, services, and products
- A demand for greater accountability and good governance
- More active and vocal stakeholders, including employees, customers, clients, and citizens
- Heightened (sometimes staggering) uncertainty about the future and significant new concerns in the face of the terrorist attacks of September 11, 2001
- Pressures to *reinvent* or *reengineer* themselves; to constantly improve the efficiency, effectiveness, and quality of their processes; and to collaborate or compete more effectively to better serve key external or internal customers
- The need to integrate plans of many different kinds—strategic, business, budget, information technology, human resource management, and financial plans, as well as short-term action plans

■ Greater difficulty in acquiring the resources they need to fulfill their missions

Leaders and managers of organizations and communities must think and act strategically, now and in the future, if they are to meet their legal, ethical, and professional obligations successfully. The tool of strategic planning is a must if these organizations and communities are to compete, survive, and prosper—and if real public value is to be created and the common good is to be served.

This workbook addresses key issues in the design of an overall strategic planning process from the initial stages through subsequent implementation, review, and evaluation. However, it only touches on the major elements of these processes. We therefore recommend that this workbook be used in tandem with the third edition of *Strategic Planning for Public and Nonprofit Organizations* (Bryson, 2004), which places the workbook's guidance and worksheets in a broader context, provides information on other significant issues, reviews relevant details, and alerts users to important caveats.

Furthermore, this workbook is not a substitute for the internal or external professional strategic planning consultation and facilitation services that are often needed during a strategic planning effort. The process of strategic planning is both important enough and difficult enough that having support from someone who has "been there and done that" may make the difference between a successful, high-value effort and one that stalls or fails or even though completed does not produce high-value results.

Audience

This workbook is intended mostly for leaders, managers, planners, employees, and other stakeholders of public and nonprofit organizations and communities. We have found, however, that many people in private sector organizations have used the first edition of this workbook too, either because their organizations have a direct business relationship with public or nonprofit organizations or because they find the approach generally applicable to organizational strategic planning. We have also discovered that a surprising number of people use this approach to do personal strategic planning, that is, for themselves as individuals. The audience for the second edition of this workbook therefore includes

People interested in exploring the applicability of strategic planning to themselves or to their organizations, networks, or communities

Sponsors, champions, and funders of strategic planning processes
Strategic planning teams
Strategic planning consultants and process facilitators
Teachers and students of strategic planning

Where This Workbook Will Be Relevant

This workbook is designed to be of use to a variety of people and groups:

Organizations as a whole
Parts of organizations (departments, divisions, offices, bureaus, units)
Programs, projects, business processes, and functions (such as personnel, finance, purchasing, information management) that cross departmental lines within an organization
Programs, projects, business processes, and services that involve more than one organization
Networks or groups of organizations
Communities
On occasion, single individuals

The worksheets generally assume that the focus of the strategic planning effort is an organization. Please tailor and modify them appropriately if your focus is different.

How This Workbook Facilitates Strategic Planning

The strategic planning process is "demystified" and made understandable and accessible. Although we have taken the risk of simplifying a complex process, this approach has been tested in hundreds of strategic planning efforts.
Fears about the process are allayed through the presentation of a simple, flexible model; step-by-step guidance; and easily understood worksheets.
Process sponsors, champions, consultants, and facilitators are provided with many of the tools they will need to guide an organization or group through a strategic process of thought and action.
The complex process of strategic planning has been broken down into manageable steps.
Use of the workbook can document progress and keep the process on track.

Communication among process participants is made easier by the workbook's structured approach.

Tangible products emerge from use of the worksheets, including those necessary to develop a strategic plan. These products can guide the discussion and the process and substantiate the need for important changes.

Overview of the Contents

This workbook is divided into two sections:

- Part One presents an overview of the strategic planning and implementation process and the benefits to be gained by using it. The chapter on the context and process of strategic change includes readiness assessment worksheets.
- Part Two covers each of the ten key steps of the process in more detail. Each step description includes sections on purpose and possible desired planning outcomes and offers worksheets to facilitate the process.

The book ends with supportive resources, a glossary, and a bibliography.

Acknowledgments

John would like to thank all the people with whom he has worked over the years on various strategic planning projects. He has learned so much from them and appreciates their willingness to help him understand more about strategic planning and how to make it more effective. He would also like to thank all the people who have taken his classes and workshops in strategic planning. They have helped him understand how best to teach strategic planning. And he is especially appreciative of Farnum Alston's contribution and his willingness to bring his enormous experience and talent to bear on this workbook project. In addition to providing many of the ideas reflected throughout, Farnum has field-tested this workbook in a wide variety of settings. Finally, John would like to thank Barbara Crosby, for her special insights, constant encouragement, and love throughout the process of developing the second edition of this workbook, and his beloved and wonderful children, Kee and Jessica.

Farnum would like to thank the many colleagues, clients, and friends who have contributed to this revised workbook. Their involvement in the hands-on process of improving public and private governance in over 300 strategic planning and management projects over the last eight years has added greatly to this revision. He would specifically like to acknowledge Susan Forman, John Gavares, Carole Jones, Dave Schwartz, Dale Stanway, and Michael Wright. Special thanks go to John Bryson for his friendship and easy collaboration, which has now spanned nearly thirty years. His significant contributions to improving public and private sector leadership have assisted all of us. Finally, Farnum's deepest gratitude goes to his wife, Kirsten Alston, his "copilot" in life, and to their daughter, Greer, for their love and support.

August 2004

John M. Bryson
Minneapolis, Minnesota

Farnum K. Alston
San Anselmo, California

The Authors

John M. Bryson is professor of planning and public affairs at the Hubert H. Humphrey Institute of Public Affairs at the University of Minnesota. He received his B.A. degree (1969) in economics from Cornell University and three degrees from the University of Wisconsin, Madison: his M.A. degree (1972) in public policy and administration, his M.S. degree (1974) in urban and regional planning, and his Ph.D. degree (1978) in urban and regional planning. In addition to publishing over eighty scholarly articles and book chapters, he is the author of the best-selling *Strategic Planning for Public and Nonprofit Organizations,* now in its third edition (Jossey-Bass, 2004). The Public and Nonprofit Sector Division of the Academy of Management named that book's second edition the Best Book of 1995. He is the coauthor, with Barbara C. Crosby, of *Leadership for the Common Good* (Jossey-Bass, 1992), which received the 1993 Terry McAdam Book Award from the Nonprofit Management Association "for outstanding contribution to the advancement of the nonprofit sector" and was also named Best Book of 1992 by the Public and Nonprofit Sector Division of the Academy of Management. A second edition of *Leadership for the Common Good* will be published by Jossey-Bass in 2005. He is also the coauthor, with Fran Ackermann, Colin Eden, and Charles Finn, of *Visible Thinking: Unlocking Causal Mapping for Practical Business Results* (Wiley, 2004).

Bryson is a recipient of the General Electric Award for Outstanding Research in Strategic Planning from the Academy of Management, along with numerous other academic awards. He has served as a consultant to a wide range of public, nonprofit, and for-profit organizations in North America and Europe.

Farnum K. Alston is founder and president of The Crescent Company (TCC), 218 Crescent Road, San Anselmo, California 94960; phone: (415) 927-2000; fax: (415) 927-1008; e-mail: farnumalston@worldnet.att.net. The Crescent Company specializes in assisting public and private sector clients with business management and planning projects. Alston has conducted over 350 major strategic planning and management projects over the last thirty years for public and private clients in the United States and Canada.

Alston has had hands-on experience in both the public and private sectors. He has served as deputy mayor and budget director in the City and County of San Francisco for then mayor Dianne Feinstein, staff director of the federal Upper Great Lakes Regional Commission, adviser to former Wisconsin governor Patrick Lucey, a partner at KPMG Peat Marwick and director of that firm's strategic planning practice, and president of The Resources Company. He completed his undergraduate work at the University of California, Berkeley, and did postgraduate work at Montana State University, Bozeman, and at the University of Wisconsin, Madison.

Creating
and
Implementing
Your
Strategic Plan

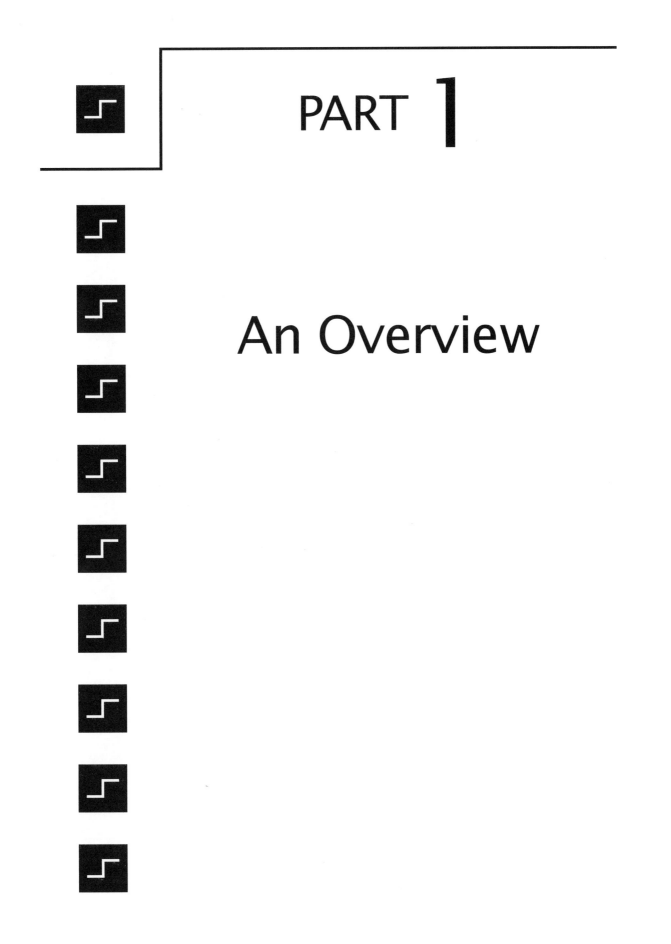

PART 1

An Overview

Introduction

■ What Is Strategic Planning and Why Do It?

Strategic planning is "a disciplined effort to produce fundamental decisions and actions that shape and guide what an organization (or other entity) is, what it does, and why it does it" (Bryson, 2004).

All organizations are in a constant state of change and flux—even those that think of themselves as static. People are coming and going, mandates are shifting, budgets are changing, stakeholder needs and expectations are changing, and so on. A strategically managed organization is one that both defines where it wants to be and manages change through an action agenda to achieve that future.

- Strategic planning is a way of thinking, acting, and learning.
- It usually takes a comprehensive view by focusing on the "big picture," but it also leads to specific, targeted actions.
- It is often visionary and usually proactive rather than reactive.
- It is flexible and practical.
- It is a guide for decision making and resource allocation.

Strategic planning is also not one thing but a set of concepts, procedures, and tools that can help public and nonprofit organizations and communities become more successful in achieving their mission or vision and creating public value.

Through strategic planning organizations can

- Document and discuss the environment in which they exist and operate, and explore the factors and trends that affect the way they do business and carry out their roles.
- Clarify and frame the issues or challenges facing the organization.
- Clarify organizational goals, and articulate a vision for where the organization wants to be.
- Develop strategies to meet their mandates, fulfill their missions, and create public value by reexamining and reworking organizational mandates, mission and values, product or service level and mix, clients, users or payers, cost, financing, structure, processes, or management.

To be effective, strategic planning must be action oriented and must be linked to tactical and operational planning. It also must be linked to a variety of *functional* types of planning, including information technology, human resource, financing, and business plans.

■ Several Complementary Ways of Looking at and Thinking About Strategic Planning

Strategic planning is a process that typically results in a plan—and the process itself needs to be thought about strategically and often planned as well. We have developed several complementary ways of viewing strategic planning, in order to both describe the process and help people understand what is involved. Different people resonate with different views. These views are

The ABCs of strategic planning
The building-block view
The strategic planning process cycle
The project management view
The Strategy Change Cycle (presented in the next chapter)
The creating public value view (presented in the next chapter)

The ABCs of Strategic Planning

Throughout its strategic planning process an organization must ask itself three fundamental questions (Figure 1):

Figure 1 ■ The ABCs of Strategic Planning

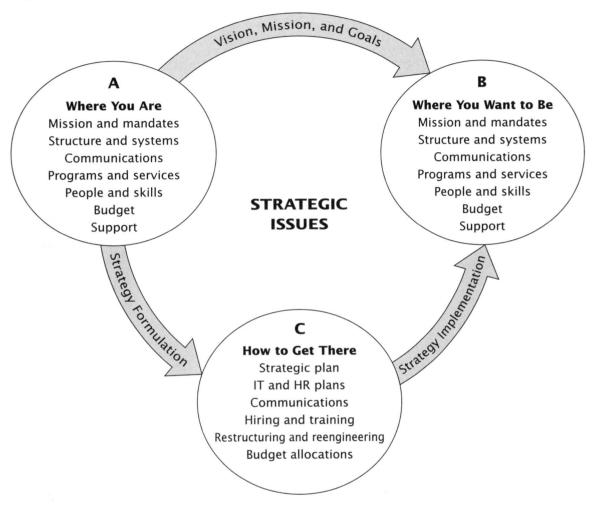

A. Who and what are we, what do we do now, and why?

The answers to the first question document the organization's current condition and establish the baseline from which to develop the strategic plan. Planning process participants often think they already know all this information, but when the question is explored and the answers are documented in a systematic way, participants almost invariably find they didn't know it all, much is learned, and many new insights emerge. Just as preliminary thinking about form and function affects the quality of the foundation of a building, the better the job you do in exploring this question at the start of your planning effort, the better the foundation for the overall plan will be.

B. What do we want to be and do in the future, and why?

The second question puts a stake in the ground. It asks, where do we and other stakeholders want to be in the future, given where we are now? Yogi Berra said, "You've got to be very careful if you don't know where you're going, because you might not get there." A strategically managed organization takes a different tack when its members identify a desired direction and proactively work together to get there.

C. How do we get from here to there?

This question answers the question of how we close the gap between where we are and where we want to be. The gap consists of the strategic issues the organization needs to address. The issues are addressed by formulating and implementing strategies and actions that respond effectively to the issues.

Asking and answering these questions requires an ongoing, iterative conversation among strategic planning team members and other key stakeholders. As the conversation unfolds, new answers to one question can be expected to change previous answers to other questions. The ten-step process and the worksheets presented in this workbook provide a reasonable and structured approach to answering these questions.

The Building-Block View

Although a strategic planning process can start at several places, we have found that a visual model is helpful in presenting the elements—or *building blocks*—of a strategic planning process and plan and the phases that most processes go through (Figure 2).

Although the building blocks generally fit together logically within the phases, several different building blocks from different phases may be worked on at any one time.

The four phases are

1. Organizing the planning process and analyzing the environment
2. Identifying and analyzing strategic issues
3. Developing strategies and action plans
4. Implementing strategies

Each of these four general phases consists of several building blocks of project activity and information that will result in a specific planning product.

Figure 2 ■ The Building-Block View of Strategic Planning

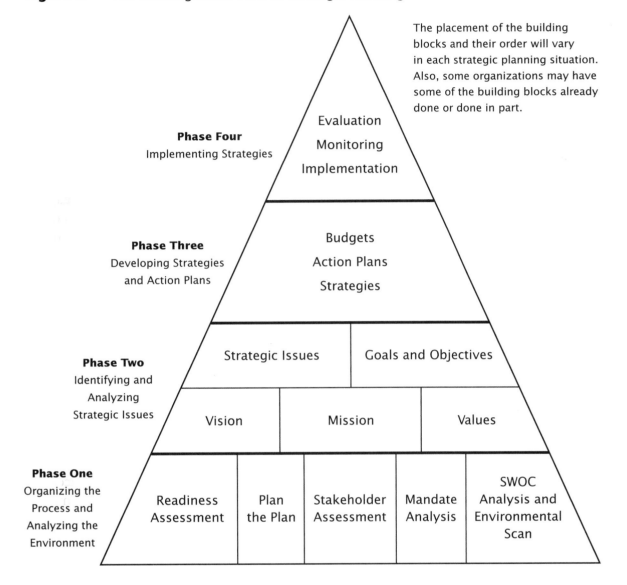

The placement of the building blocks and their order will vary in each strategic planning situation. Also, some organizations may have some of the building blocks already done or done in part.

Phase Four
Implementing Strategies

Evaluation
Monitoring
Implementation

Phase Three
Developing Strategies
and Action Plans

Budgets
Action Plans
Strategies

Phase Two
Identifying and
Analyzing
Strategic Issues

Strategic Issues | Goals and Objectives

Vision | Mission | Values

Phase One
Organizing the
Process and
Analyzing the
Environment

Readiness Assessment | Plan the Plan | Stakeholder Assessment | Mandate Analysis | SWOC Analysis and Environmental Scan

Although some organizations may have some of these building blocks in place already, we have found that revisiting and documenting them within a structured strategic planning process is extremely helpful—particularly when the process involves new participants. For example, many organizations are convinced they already know what their mission and mandates are now and should be in the future. Our experience, however, is quite different. Typically, a large fraction of the organization's stakeholders display considerable ambiguity about or even ignorance of the mission and mandates.

In phase 1 the foundation is laid for the overall strategic plan itself:

■ Readiness assessment

In conducting a readiness assessment the organization explores its capacity to do a strategic planning process. We have assisted many clients who got into a planning process without conducting an appropriate readiness assessment and ended up trying to use a hammer when they needed a saw. It is important to be candid and ask the tough organizational questions before embarking on a strategic planning project.

■ Plan the plan

The time spent on planning the plan is almost always well spent. As with building a home, you need to think the process through. Take the time to do this part of the process carefully, and it will pay off many times over the course of the project.

■ Stakeholder assessment
■ Mandate analysis
■ Assessment of internal strengths and weaknesses and external opportunities and challenges

Phase 2 establishes a clear sense of direction for the organization, as planners look at

■ Vision, mission, and values
■ Strategic issues, goals, and objectives

Phase 3 shows in more detail how the organization will address the issues it faces and build effective bridges from itself to its environment via

■ Strategies
■ Action plans
■ Budgets

Phase 4 is where the ultimate payoffs are achieved and assessed, through

■ Implementation
■ Monitoring
■ Evaluation

The Strategic Planning Process Cycle

The building-block view of strategic planning will seem too static for some. The cyclical nature of strategic planning is shown in Figure 3. The cycle is organized around an evolving sense of who the stakeholders are and what they want and of the vision and goals, and it involves

- Planning the process
- Establishing mission and mandates and assessing the internal and external environment
- Identifying strategic issues
- Formulating strategies and an action agenda
- Reviewing and adopting a strategic plan
- Implementing and reassessing the plan
- Beginning the cycle anew

The Project Management View

Strategic planning may also be thought of in operational terms, because it is often conceived and organized as a *project*. Exhibit 1 presents a list of tasks and timelines for implementing an action that strategic planning has identified.

Two other views of strategic planning are presented in the next chapter. The Strategy Change Cycle is the ten-step process used to organize this workbook. The creating public value view shows how those ten steps can contribute to creating public value.

■ The Benefits of Strategic Planning

Strategic planning is intended to enhance an organization's ability to think, act, and learn strategically. The potential benefits from the process are numerous, although there is no guarantee that they will be realized in practice. These benefits include

- *Increased effectiveness.* The organization's performance is enhanced, its mission is furthered, its mandates are met, and real public value is created. In addition, the organization responds effectively to rapidly changing circumstances.
- *Increased efficiency.* The same or better results are achieved with fewer resources.
- *Improved understanding and better learning.* The organization understands its situation far more clearly. It is able to reconceptualize

Figure 3 ■ The Strategic Planning Process Cycle

The strategic planning process is typically cyclical and can begin at many places.

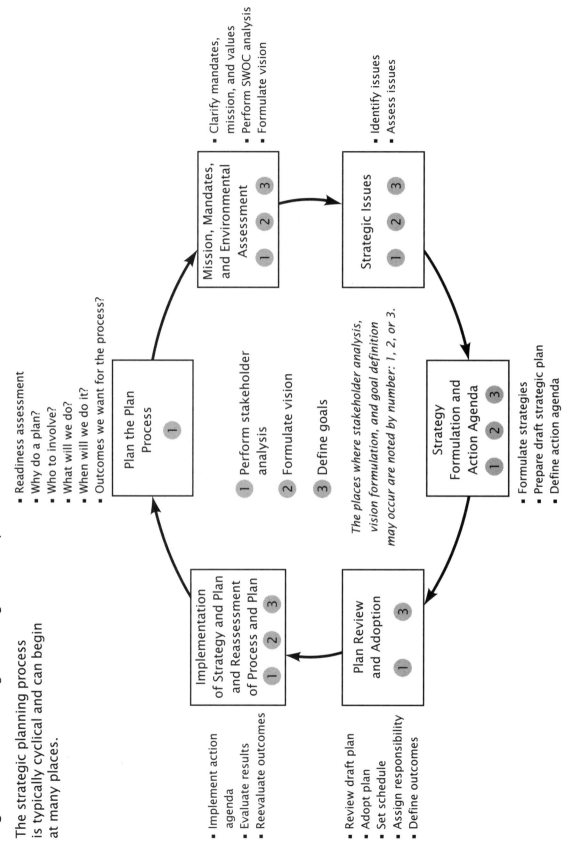

- Readiness assessment
- Why do a plan?
- Who to involve?
- What will we do?
- When will we do it?
- Outcomes we want for the process?

Plan the Plan Process
1

Mission, Mandates, and Environmental Assessment
1 2 3

- Clarify mandates, mission, and values
- Perform SWOC analysis
- Formulate vision

Strategic Issues
1 2 3

- Identify issues
- Assess issues

1 Perform stakeholder analysis

2 Formulate vision

3 Define goals

The places where stakeholder analysis, vision formulation, and goal definition may occur are noted by number: 1, 2, or 3.

Strategy Formulation and Action Agenda
1 2 3

- Formulate strategies
- Prepare draft strategic plan
- Define action agenda

Implementation of Strategy and Plan and Reassessment of Process and Plan
1 2 3

- Implement action agenda
- Evaluate results
- Reevaluate outcomes

Plan Review and Adoption
1 3

- Review draft plan
- Adopt plan
- Set schedule
- Assign responsibility
- Define outcomes

Exhibit 1 ■ The Project Management View of Strategic Planning: Example of Implementing an Action

Action	Key Steps or Tasks	Due Dates	Responsible Party and Involved Parties	Resources and Outcomes		
				People	Funding	Measurable Outcomes
1. Educate department managers and staff on the roles and responsibilities of the ABC organization's strategy	a. Update educational materials	Jan. 24	Organization training manager, ABC trainer, department trainers	.5 PY time	Printing costs	Document produced
	b. Determine date for 1 day of training	Feb. 4	ABC program trainer, department reps	Book facilitation help, room, and 20 people for the day	Meeting room and materials NA	Date established and facilities and facilitator booked
	c. Design the 1-day training event	Feb. 10	ABC trainer	3 days' effort	NA	Meeting design
	d. Hold training event	Feb. 24	ABC trainer and department helpers	1-day meeting	NA	Training held and evaluations are positive
	e. Follow-up	Mar. 2	ABC trainer and organization management	2 hours ABC trainer and senior managers		Good meeting and process assessment; action plans for having another training session if needed

its situation and work, if necessary, and to establish an interpretive framework that can guide strategy development and implementation.

- *Better decision making.* A coherent, focused, and defensible basis for decision making is established, and today's decisions are made in light of their future consequences.
- *Enhanced organizational capabilities.* Broadly based organizational leadership is improved, and the capacity for further strategic thought, action, and learning is enhanced.
- *Improved communications and public relations.* Mission, vision, goals, strategies, and action programs are communicated more effectively to key stakeholders. A desirable image for the organization is established and managed.
- *Increased political support.* The organization's legitimacy is enhanced, its advocacy base broadened, and a powerful and supportive coalition developed.

■ Poor Excuses for Avoiding Strategic Planning

A number of reasons can be offered for not engaging in strategic planning. Too often, however, these "reasons" are actually excuses for avoiding necessary action. For example:

- *We don't have policy board support.* Think strategically about how to gain this board's support, perhaps for an effort aimed at addressing a single issue.
- *There's no top management support.* Again, think strategically about how to win management support.
- *Strategic planning won't lead to perfection.* Of course it won't!
- *We're too big (or too small) for strategic planning.* If the U.S. Navy, the Internal Revenue Service, and the smallest nonprofits can benefit from strategic planning—which they do—size is not a legitimate argument for avoiding it.
- *We've got a union.* Then treat the union as another stakeholder.
- *We have personnel policies and individual performance goals to take care of this.* Think strategically about personnel policies, and ask whether or not the individual performance goals support desirable organizational strategies.
- *We don't know where to start.* You can start anywhere. The process is so interconnected that you will find yourselves covering most phases through conversation and dialogue no matter where you start.

- *We've already done it*—years ago. Times change. Revisit what you've done to see if it is still relevant.
- *We're perfect already!* Then you *really* need to be careful, because nothing breeds failure like success and the complacency that often comes with it.

■ Two Legitimate Reasons Not to Undertake Strategic Planning

Strategic planning is not always advisable for an organization. There are two compelling reasons for holding off on a strategic planning effort:

1. Strategic planning may not be the best first step for an organization whose roof has fallen. For example, the organization may need to remedy a cash flow crunch or fill a key leadership position before undertaking strategic planning.
2. If the organization lacks the skills or resources or the commitment of key decision makers to carry through an effective strategic planning process and produce a good plan, the effort should not be undertaken. If strategic planning is attempted in such a situation, it should probably be a focused and limited effort aimed at developing those skills, resources, and commitments.

The Context and Process of Strategic Change

■ The Strategy Change Cycle: An Effective Strategic Planning Approach for Public and Nonprofit Organizations

This workbook is organized around a strategic planning and implementation process, the Strategy Change Cycle, that has proved effective for many public and nonprofit organizations. The Strategy Change Cycle is designed to help organizations meet their mandates, fulfill their missions, and create public value. The ten steps of the cycle are presented in Figure 4. The steps are as follows:

STEP | 1   Initiate and Agree on a Strategic Planning Process

The purpose of step 1 is to negotiate agreement with key internal (and possibly external) decision makers or opinion leaders on the overall strategic planning process, the schedule, and the key planning tasks.

15

Figure 4 ■ The Strategy Change Cycle

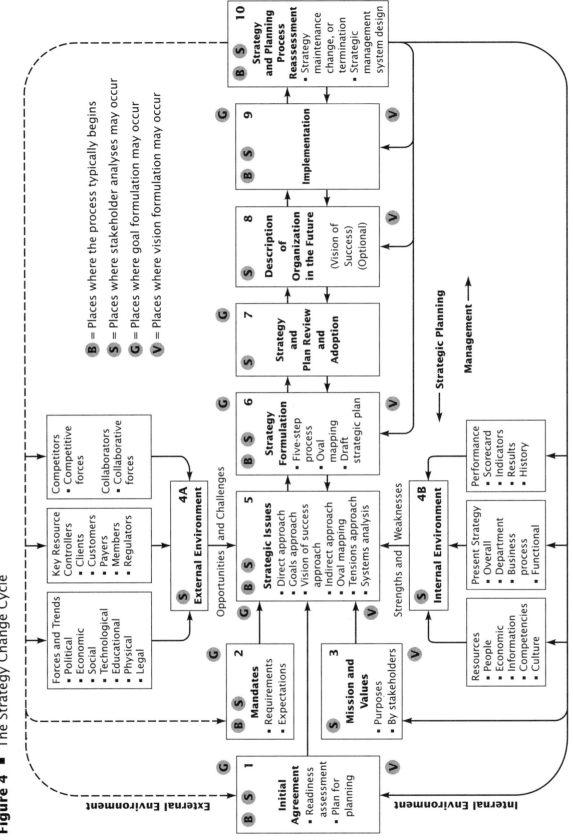

Some person or group must initiate the process. One of this person's or group's first important tasks is to identify the key decision makers. The next is to determine which persons, groups, units, or organizations should be involved in the effort. The initial agreement will be negotiated with at least some of these decision makers, groups, units, or organizations.

Before a strategic planning effort is begun, however, it may be useful to perform a readiness assessment. The purpose of such an assessment is to determine how capable the organization is of undertaking a strategic planning effort and whether additional capacity may be needed. See Worksheets 1 through 5 at the end of this chapter. (Sample questionnaires for performing more elaborate assessments of the internal and external environments are presented in Resources E and F.)

The strategic planning process agreement itself should cover

- The purpose of the effort
- Preferred steps in the process
- The schedule
- The form and timing of reports
- The role, functions, and membership of any group or committee empowered to oversee the effort
- The role, functions, and membership of the strategic planning team
- Commitment of resources necessary to proceed with the effort

See Worksheet 6.

STEP 2 Clarify Organizational Mandates

The purpose of this step is to clarify the formal and informal mandates placed on the organization (the *musts* it confronts) and to explore their implications for organizational action.

See Worksheets 7 and 8.

STEP 3 Identify and Understand Stakeholders and Develop and Refine Mission and Values

A stakeholder is any person, group, or entity that can place a claim on the organization's attention, resources, or output or that is affected by that output. The key to success for public and nonprofit organizations is the ability to address the needs of crucial stakeholders—according to those stakeholders' criteria.

The organization's mission, in tandem with its mandates, provides its raison d'être and its principal route to creating public value. Any government, corporation, agency, or nonprofit organization must seek to meet certain identifiable social or political needs. Viewed in this light, an organization must always be considered the means to an end, not an end in and of itself.

The mission statement developed and refined in this step should grow out of a thorough consideration of who the organization's (or community's) stakeholders are. The organization's value system might also be identified, discussed, and documented. The organization may also wish to create a sketch of its *vision of success,* to guide subsequent planning efforts.

See Worksheets 9 through 16.

STEP | 4   Assess the Environment to Identify Strengths, Weaknesses, Opportunities, and Challenges

In this step the strengths and weaknesses of the organization are catalogued and evaluated and their strategic implications noted. This may include identifying the organization's distinctive competencies—that is, those abilities that enable it to perform well against key performance indicators (or critical success factors), especially when compared to its competitors. In addition, the opportunities and challenges (or threats) facing the organization are explored, and again, strategic implications are recognized.

See Worksheets 17 through 21.

STEP | 5   Identify and Frame Strategic Issues

Together, the first four steps of the process lead to the fifth, the identification of strategic issues—the fundamental challenges affecting the organization's mandates, its mission and values, its product or service level and mix, its costs, its financing, its structure, its processes, and its management.

See Worksheets 22 through 25.

STEP | 6   Formulate Strategies to Manage the Issues

Strategies are developed to deal with the issues identified in step 5. Strategies may be of several types:

- Grand strategy for the organization, network, or community as a whole
- Strategy for organizational subunits
- Program, service, product, or business process strategies

■ Strategies for functions such as human resource management, information technology, finance, and purchasing

These strategies can be used to set the context for other change efforts aimed at "reinventing the organization," "reengineering the organization," "process improvement and management projects," "competition or collaboration," and so on.

See Worksheets 26 through 29.

Steps 1 through 6 may be thought of as strategic *planning,* whereas steps 7 through 10 are more about *management.* All the steps together may be thought of as a *strategic management process.*

STEP 7 Review and Adopt the Strategic Plan

The purpose of this step is to gain a formal commitment to adopt and proceed with implementation of the plan(s). This step represents the culmination of the work of the previous steps and points toward the implementation step, in which adopted strategies are realized in practice. Formal adoption may not be necessary in all cases to gain the benefits of strategic planning, but quite often it is.

See Worksheets 30 and 31.

STEP 8 Establish an Effective Organizational Vision for the Future

An organization's vision of success outlines what the organization should look like as it successfully implements its strategies and achieves its full potential. Such a description, to the extent that it is widely known and agreed on in the organization, allows organizational members to know what is expected of them without constant direct managerial oversight. This description also allows other key stakeholders to know what the organization envisions for itself.

Visions of success may be developed at several places in the process—and worksheets in previous steps have prompted planning process participants to think about their vision for the future—but step 8 is often where it happens. Most organizations will not be able to develop an effective vision of success until they have gone through strategic planning more than once. Thus, their visions of success are more likely to serve as a guide for strategy implementation and less as a guide for strategy formulation.

See Worksheet 32.

STEP 9   Develop an Effective Implementation Process

In this step, adopted strategies are implemented throughout the relevant systems. An effective implementation process and action plan must be developed if the strategic plan is to be something other than an organizational New Year's resolution. The more that strategies have been formulated with implementation in mind and the more active the involvement of those required to implement the plan, the more successful strategy implementation is likely to be.

See Worksheets 33 through 36.

STEP 10   Reassess Strategies and the Strategic Planning Process

The purpose of the final step is to review implemented strategies and the strategic planning process. The aim is to find out what worked, what did not work, and why, and to set the stage for the next round of strategic planning.

See Worksheets 37 and 38.

■ The Strategy Change Cycle: Theory Versus Practice

Although the process has been laid out in a linear, sequential manner, it must be emphasized that in practice the process is typically iterative: participants usually rethink what they have done several times before they reach final decisions. Moreover, the process does not always begin at the beginning. Organizations may find themselves confronted with a serious strategic issue or a failing strategy that leads them to engage in strategic planning, and only later do they do step 1.

It is also important to note that strategic planning efforts necessarily take place within a given context, even if the purpose of the effort is to change the context. Unless strategic planning is being used to design a brand-new organization, it will occur within ongoing processes of organizational change (which are typically cyclical or nonlinear) and must fit those processes. They include budgeting cycles, legislative cycles, decision-making routines of the governing board, and other change initiatives. Among the elements that may be involved are process improvement initiatives, information technology upgrades, and personnel system reform.

There are also different levels of organizational change, ranging from the more abstract or conceptual (such as changes in mission, vision, and general goals) to the more specific or concrete (such as changes in work plans and budgets). Change may be orchestrated from the top, proceeding "deductively" down to the more concrete and specific level, or change may be initiated at the more concrete level, rising "inductively" toward the more abstract or conceptual level. Most often, change involves a combination of deductive and inductive approaches, and these must be blended as wisely as possible (Mintzberg and Westley, 1992; Mintzberg, Ahlstrand, and Lampel, 1998).

It is extremely important to note that, as indicated in Figure 4, goal formulation and visioning activities may be inserted at many points in the process, depending on the circumstances. As often as not, goal formulation comes later in the process, when strategies are formulated. Goals developed there will be reflected in the thrusts of specific strategies. Goals agreed on earlier in the process may well be too vague to serve as useful guides for action. Nonetheless, if agreement can be reached earlier on reasonably specific and detailed goals, they may be used to guide the initial work of the process, to facilitate the framing of strategic issues, or to direct strategy formulation efforts. Similarly, a vision of success typically is developed toward the end of the process, to guide implementation, but under certain circumstances may be prepared earlier. As with goals, visioning activities can be used to guide the planning process from the beginning or to frame strategic issues; they can also help in the development of strategies.

■ Key Design Choices

A number of interconnected design choices must be made to enhance the prospects for a successful strategic planning process. These choices are some of the most important decisions organizations make when it comes to strategic planning. Some of the more important choices are

- Whose plan is it?
    Is the plan to be "owned" by a community, organization, organizational unit, program, project, or function?
    What are the implications of this choice for participation?
- What are the purposes of the strategic planning effort?
    In what ways are the planning process and the plan intended to enhance organizational or community performance and create public value?
    What other benefits of strategic planning are sought?
    What values should the process itself embody in the way it is organized and pursued?
- How will the process be tailored to the situation at hand?
    Has strategic planning been attempted before—successfully or unsuccessfully?

Are goal formulation and visioning activities necessary, and if so, where will they occur in the process?

Which approach to the identification of strategic issues will be used?

How will the process fit with other ongoing organizational processes and change efforts, such as budgeting cycles or process improvement and information technology initiatives?

How will the process be tailored to fit the organization's culture—even if that culture is one of the objects of change?

- How will the process be managed?

Who will sponsor and empower the process?

Who will manage the process? Who will the internal process managers—the process champions—be?

How will the process be broken down into phases, activities, and tasks?

What is the project time frame?

What kind of consultation and facilitation will be needed?

How will the process accommodate commitments from sponsors and participants in terms of time, energy, and financial and political resources?

■ What Are the Dangers to Avoid?

There are many ways in which strategic planning can fail. Without broad sponsorship, careful and skilled management, adequate resources, excellent timing, and a fair measure of luck, the process may fail. Whenever you ask people to focus in a serious way on what is fundamental and to consider doing things differently, you threaten the organization's existing culture, coalitions, values, and interaction patterns. Anger, rage, frustration, and rejection of the process may result, no matter how necessary the process may be to ensure organizational survival and prosperity.

There is also an inherent skepticism and resistance to strategic planning among line managers, who have a strong operational orientation—"What will this do for me?"

■ What Are the Keys to a Successful Process?

In many ways the keys to success are the mirror image of the potential sources of failure:

Be sure the organization is ready. Conduct a readiness assessment. If the organization is not prepared, identify capacity problems and focus thought and action on remedying them. Use Worksheets 1 through 5 (and perhaps Resources E and F) to assist you in determining whether your organization is ready for strategic planning.

Strengthen leadership and ensure adequate participation by key stakeholders. You will need strong sponsors and the support of key stakeholders throughout the process. Include major decision makers, managers, opinion leaders, and other stakeholders essential to the success of the effort. Make sure they are willing to devote the time needed to discuss what is truly important for the organization and to act on what they learn.

Make sure the process has a skillful champion (or champions). Sponsors provide the authority and power to initiate, carry out, and legitimize the process. But sponsors are typically not involved in managing the process on a day-to-day basis—the champion is. You need a champion who understands the process and is committed to it. Note that champions are not committed to specific issues and strategies; they are committed to getting key people together to focus on what is important and to do something about it.

Build understanding to support wise strategic thinking, acting, and learning. Clearly communicate the purposes of the process to key stakeholders. Engage in the analysis and discussions required to build adequate understanding of the organization, its circumstances, and its potential strategic choices. Manage expectations so that neither too much nor too little is expected of the process. Take the time and allocate the resources to "do it right."

Cultivate necessary political support. Sponsorship by key decision makers is typically crucial to the success of a strategic planning effort. Beyond that, a coalition of supporters must be built that is large enough and strong enough to adopt the strategic plan and support it during implementation.

Foster effective decision making and implementation. Help decision makers focus on the truly important issues. Link the strategic plan to resource allocation decisions. Develop an implementation process and action planning effort that will ensure the realization of adopted strategies, and link these processes to operational plans and to resource allocation decisions.

Design a process that is likely to succeed. Build on existing planning, management, and other change efforts and routines, while still keeping the strategic planning process unique and special. Fit the process to the situation at hand. Fit the process to the organization's (or community's) culture. Use the process to inform key decisions. Be realistic about the scope and scale of the strategic planning agenda. Find a way to accommodate the day-to-day demands on people's time. Make sure that people see the process as genuinely helpful.

Manage the process effectively. Commit the resources necessary for a successful effort. Draw on people who are skilled in the process of strategic planning.

■ The Functions and Purposes
of Strategic Planning and Management
and the Steps of the Strategy Change Cycle

Figure 5 presents the final view of strategic planning. It shows how the
steps of the Strategy Change Cycle are designed to help an organization fulfill four functions and three purposes. The overall purpose of
strategic planning and management is to create public value, chiefly
through helping the organization fulfill its mission and meet its mandates. In order to do this the organization needs to produce fundamental decisions and actions that shape and guide what the organization is,
what it does, and why it does it—the very definition of strategic planning. Effective strategic planning depends on four key, interconnected
functions being performed well: organizing participation, formulating
ideas of strategic significance, organizing a coalition to adopt the ideas,
and effectively implementing the ideas.

Figure 5 ■ Strategic Planning Purposes and Functions and Strategy Change Cycle Steps

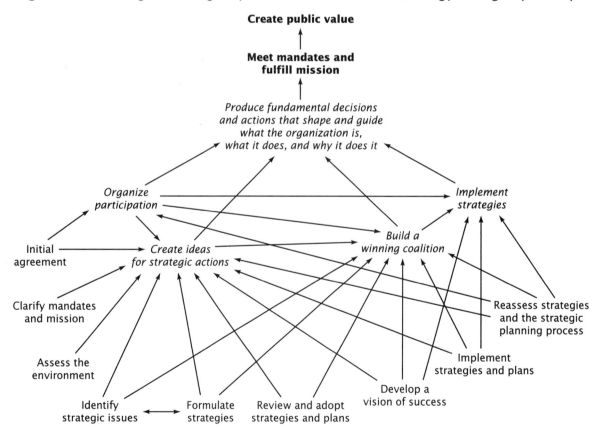

Readiness Assessment WORKSHEETS

■ Readiness Assessment Worksheet Directions

1. Someone must initiate the process of readiness assessment. This person may not necessarily be either a process sponsor or champion, but he or she should be willing to explore, in a candid and constructive way, the usefulness of strategic planning for the organization (or community).

2. Consider involving two different kinds of stakeholders at some point in the process of readiness assessment. The first might be called *process* stakeholders—people who need to be involved in some way for the process to be successful. They may or may not have much impact on the organization's issue agenda, but their involvement and support are necessary to legitimize the process and any resulting plan. The second might be called *agenda* stakeholders—people or organizations such as clients, customers, funders, regulators, or others that have a significant influence on the agenda of issues and concerns to which the organization must attend. In general, people should be involved in readiness assessment either because they have information that cannot be gained in any other way or because their support for the process and for dealing with the issues that are likely to arise will be crucial (Thomas, 1995).

3. Have participants fill out Worksheets 1 through 4 and discuss the results. (You might also consider conducting a broader survey of internal and external stakeholders, using the questionnaires in Resources E and F, or you may choose to consider using these surveys in step 4, assessing the environment to identify strengths, weaknesses, opportunities, and challenges.)

4. Have participants fill out Worksheet 5 and discuss the results.

5. Decide whether it makes sense to

    Move forward with a strategic planning effort at this time.

    Wait for a more propitious time.

    Address key organizational weaknesses first, before moving ahead with strategic planning.

WORKSHEET 1　## Strengths, Weaknesses, Opportunities, and Challenges (or Threats)

Instructions: The "readiness" or capacity of an organization to undertake a strategic planning process successfully should be clearly understood by the organization and its leaders before the process is begun. Organizational barriers to success should be identified and evaluated, and a plan or strategy should be developed to address them. (See Worksheet 2.)

The following organizational areas should be explored through interviews, focus groups, or the use of tailored questionnaires: mission and vision; budget, human resources, and information technology; communications; and leadership, management, structure, processes, and culture.

I. Mission and Vision

Successful organizations possess a clear understanding of their mandates, and they have established and communicated an inspiring organizational mission and/or vision to their stakeholders.

Please comment on any significant organizational strengths, weaknesses, opportunities, or challenges in the areas of mission and vision.

II. Budget, Human Resources, and Information Technology

Successful organizations and managers achieve their mandates, fulfill their mission, and create public value by effectively managing their resources.

Please comment on any significant organizational strengths, weaknesses, opportunities, or challenges in the areas of budget, human resources, and information technology.

III. Communications

Successful organizations transmit clear messages, have well-developed communication networks, and have adequate forums to promote discussion and dialogue. *Messages* are concise, targeted toward specific stakeholders, and designed to produce specific responses. *Networks* effectively convey appropriate information to targeted stakeholders, both internal and external. *Forums* engage appropriate stakeholders in appropriate ways to foster necessary discussion and dialogue.

Please comment on any significant organizational strengths, weaknesses, opportunities, or challenges in the area of communications.

IV. Leadership, Management, Structure, Processes, and Culture

Successful organizations enjoy effective leadership and competent management and organize themselves strategically. *Leadership* means making sure that the organization is doing the right things. *Management* means making sure that those things are being done right. The organization's *structure* should feature well-defined relationships horizontally and vertically, formally and informally, which will help the organization carry out specific strategic initiatives. The organization's *processes* should be designed to produce desired outputs efficiently and effectively. The organization's *culture* should foster a commitment to the mission, meeting the mandates, creating public value, and satisfying key stakeholders.

Please comment on any significant organizational strengths, weaknesses, opportunities, or challenges in the areas of leadership, management, structure, processes, and culture.

WORKSHEET **2**   **Barriers to Strategic Planning**

Instructions: On the basis of what you learned in completing Worksheet 1, what do you see as the *major barriers* to a successful strategic planning process? (*Examples:* lack of leadership, communication problems, resources.) How can these barriers be addressed?

Barriers	Ways They Can Be Addressed

WORKSHEET 3   Expected Costs of Strategic Planning

Instructions:

1. List the costs, direct and indirect, you expect to incur from strategic planning. (*Examples:* resources required to implement the process and plan, time required, organizational conflicts and resistance to change, other stakeholder resistance.) Note the most important of these.
2. Note ways to manage these costs.

Costs (direct and indirect)	Ways to Manage Costs

WORKSHEET **4**   **Expected Benefits of Strategic Planning**

Instructions:

1. List the benefits, direct and indirect, you expect from strategic planning. (*Examples:* better use of organization's resources, better relations with stakeholders and clients, good plan for change and change management, greater clarity about the mission.) Note the most important of these.
2. Note ways to enhance these benefits.

Benefits	Ways to Enhance Benefits

WORKSHEET 5   Should We Proceed with the Strategic Planning Process?

Instructions: Review your answers to Worksheets 1 through 4, and determine whether the following readiness criteria have been met. Then discuss the results and decide what to do next.

Readiness Criteria	Criterion Met? Yes	No
Strong process sponsor(s) has agreed to serve	☐	☐
Strong process champion(s) has agreed to serve	☐	☐
The process is within our mandate	☐	☐
Resources are available to do the planning	☐	☐
Resources are likely to be available to implement the plan	☐	☐
The process and the plan will be linked to our budgets and operational plans	☐	☐
The benefits outweigh the costs; the process will create real value for our organization and our stakeholders	☐	☐
Strategic planning is the right tool for what we need to do	☐	☐
We can figure out ways to deal with or mitigate any "No" answers to the previous questions	☐	☐
Now is the right time to initiate the process	☐	☐

Given our answers so far, should we

- Proceed   ☐ ☐
- Figure out how to change each "No" to "Yes"   ☐ ☐
- Forget about strategic planning for now   ☐ ☐

Comments:

PART 2

Creating and Implementing Strategic Planning: Ten Key Steps

STEP 1

Initiate and Agree on a Strategic Planning Process

■ Purpose of Step

The purpose of step 1 is to develop an initial agreement among key decision makers and opinion leaders about the overall strategic planning effort and main planning tasks and to authorize advocates and facilitators to move forward with the process. Certain external decision makers and opinion leaders may need to be parties to the agreement if their information or support will be essential to the success of the effort.

This initial agreement is one of the most important steps in the whole strategic planning process. In step 1, many of the commitments necessary to produce a good process and plan are developed. Among other things, these commitments define the individuals and groups that will be relied on to carry the process forward. In addition, many critical questions concerning process design are answered. For example:

- Whose plan is it?
- What are the purposes of the process and plan?
- How will the process be tailored to fit the situation?
- How will the process be managed?
- How will the process be broken down into phases or tasks?
- What schedule will be adopted?

Adequate commitments and wise process design choices are critical to a successful outcome. (Refer to the worksheet at the end of this step.)

■ Possible Desired Planning Outcomes

- Agreement on

  The worth and scope of the strategic planning effort; organizations, units, groups, or persons who should be involved or informed. Be clear about whether the planning effort is strictly an internal process or whether it will also involve external stakeholders.

  Process phases, specific tasks, activities, and schedule

  Form and timing of reports

- Formation of a strategic planning coordinating committee (SPCC) that sets process policy and direction
- Formation of a strategic planning team (SPT) that coordinates day-to-day process and plan activities and needs
- Selection of a consultant team, if necessary, of independent process and planning experts to help design and facilitate the process
- Commitment of necessary resources to begin the effort

■ Worksheet Directions

1. Locate a person or group in your organization (or community) who is willing and able to act as a *process champion*—that is, to initiate the process and act as an advocate for the strategic planning effort.

2. Clearly identify "whose" plan it is. Consider the following questions from the very beginning, and ask your SPT and SPCC as well when they have been formed:

   Who are the process sponsors and the process champions (or champion)?

   What part of the organization (or community) is the plan for? Is it needed? (*Example:* A plan may be a single strategic plan for your whole organization, or it may be a divisional or departmental plan for management only. Both are legitimate if they can address your issues and meet your objectives and expectations.)

   Who will support it?

3. Make sure that the time frames for the plan and the process are realistic. If they are too long, the plan and the process will not be relevant; if they are too short, the plan will not be strategic and the process will not allow enough time to be strategic. A two-to-five-year plan horizon and a six-to-twelve-month strategic planning process may be reasonable in many cases. Ask your team:

What information is currently available, and how valid and reliable is it?

What information do we need to generate, and how valid and reliable must it be?

What issues are driving planning needs? Are they long-term (for example, capital budgeting or major information technology investments) or short-term (for example, operations)?

How rapidly are changes occurring, and what will be the shelf-life of a plan?

How do we get the most value from the process?

4. In planning the process:

Don't underestimate the level of effort and the time required to do the job well. That does not mean that the process has to drag on, but you need to allow enough time for adequate information gathering, discussion and dialogue, decision making, and follow-through.

Match the time to the purpose, the process, and the necessary involvements of people in the process.

Allow adequate time, or don't do a strategic plan.

As one of its first tasks, the SPCC should draft a strategic planning process *charter* to which process sponsors, champions, and participants agree. The charter should be drafted in light of the understandings and agreements worked out in response to Worksheet 6. The charter should be short, and as an absolute minimum, should describe the purpose of the process.

WORKSHEET **6**   Plan the Planning Effort

---

1. Whose plan is it? (This question is key in determining the scope of the plan and who needs to be involved in the process. You might create an initial strategic planning team to develop a draft *charter* statement as a way to explore this question.) The plan is for (you may check more than one)

   ☐ The whole organization

   ☐ The whole organization, with separate plans for major divisions, units, and the like

   ☐ Part of the organization (specify division, unit, program)

   ☐ A business, human resource, or information technology function (specify)

   ☐ Internal stakeholders or both internal and external stakeholders (specify)

   ☐ Other, such an interorganizational network or community (specify)

2. What period of time will the plan cover? Keep the time horizon realistic, to avoid undermining the credibility and usefulness of the plan.

   ☐ 2 years

   ☐ 5 years

   ☐ Other (specify)

3. What challenges, issues, problems, or concerns do we hope the planning process and the plan itself will address?

4. Who is sponsoring the strategic planning process? And do they have the necessary authority and power and the resources and time?

   ☐ Senior managers

   ☐ Middle managers

   ☐ Policy board members

   ☐ Staff

   ☐ External stakeholders

   ☐ Others

5. Who is (are) or will be the process champion(s)? And does each champion have the backing of the sponsors and the ability, resources, and time?

6. Who will be on the strategic planning project team?

   ☐ Policy board members

   ☐ Senior managers

   ☐ Middle managers

   ☐ Staff

   ☐ Other stakeholders, possibly including external stakeholders

   ☐ Consultants

7. What kind and size of strategic planning team works (or will work) best in our organization? Think about who should own and be committed to the plan at the end of the process and what that means for the composition of the strategic planning team.

8. Who should be involved in the development of the plan? Again, think about who should own and be committed to the plan at the end of the process and what that means for involvement in the strategic planning effort.

9. Who should be involved in the review of the plan prior to and during any formal adoption process?

10. Who are the audiences for the plan? To whom will it be marketed?

11. How many hours are we willing to give to the strategic planning process, including meetings?

    ☐ 1–12

    ☐ 12–24

    ☐ 24–40

    ☐ 40+

12. Are we using internal or external consultants or other resource experts?

    ☐ Yes. Who will they be and what roles will they play?

    ☐ No.

    ☐ Unsure. If we are unsure, what kind of help do we think we might need?

13. How will we coordinate with and use consultants and process experts?

14. Who will manage the day-to-day planning effort?

15. What type of written plan do we envision?

    ☐ Short executive summary

    ☐ Longer and more detailed plan but not including most tactical and operational elements

    ☐ A detailed plan including tactical and operational elements

    ☐ Other

16. What is the expected time frame for the planning process?

    ☐ 6 months

    ☐ 12 months

    ☐ Other

17. What steps will we use in our planning process? Review them with the people to be involved and refine as needed. (The authors have found that programs like Microsoft's project management software are an excellent tool for project planning and tracking; see also Exhibit 1.)

Steps/Tasks	Persons/Groups Involved	Schedule

18. What resources do we need to start and to complete the effort, and where will we get them?

    ☐ Budget

    ☐ People

    ☐ Information

    ☐ Facilities for meetings

    ☐ Consultants

    ☐ Other

19. What criteria should be used to judge the effectiveness of the strategic planning process?

20. What criteria should be used to judge the effectiveness of the strategic plan?

Source: Adapted from *Strategic Planning Workbook for Nonprofit Organizations,* by Bryan W. Barry. Copyright © 1997 Amherst H. Wilder Foundation, 919 Lafond Avenue, St. Paul, Minnesota, 55104. Used with permission.

STEP 2
Clarify Organizational Mandates

■ Purpose of Step

The purpose of step 2 is to clarify the nature and meaning of externally imposed mandates that the organization is required to meet. Mandates can be expressed formally or informally. Formal mandates prescribe what must or should be done under the organization's current charter and policy and under federal, state, and local laws, codes, and regulations. Informal mandates may be embodied in election results or community or key stakeholder expectations.

As the organization sets its future course, planners need to take both formal and informal mandates into account as constraints on the goals the organization can achieve and the ways it can achieve them. It is vital that the organization have a clear understanding of its current mandates and of their implications for its actions and resources.

Having said this, we would also point out that many organizations assume they are far more constrained than they actually are. Some mandates enable a wider range of action than organizational members assume; in other words, what people think is mandated turns out not to be. Other mandates will have become dated and inappropriate. Organizational mythology needs to be reviewed, and the real mandates need to be identified, along with mandates that should be changed.

An equally common error is to overemphasize one aspect of the organization's mandates at the expense of others. For example, some organizations have support and service responsibilities as well as regulatory oversight responsibilities. The proper balance between service and support on the one hand and control and enforcement on the other hand is often an important issue. Our experience is that usually one aspect dominates the organization's culture, and so one type of mandate gets most of the attention, which may not be in either the organization's or the public's best interests.

■ Possible Desired Planning Outcomes

- Compilation of the organization's formal and informal mandates
- Interpretation of what is required by the mandates and what is not
- Clarification of what is not ruled out by the mandates
- Evaluation of whether specific mandates are dated or still viable

■ Worksheet Directions

1. Have someone compile a list of the formal and informal mandates faced by the organization (Worksheet 7).
2. Review these mandates to clarify what is required and what is allowed. Discuss the implications of the mandates for existing or potential programs, projects, and services and for resource allocations. Have individuals fill out Worksheet 8 by themselves first, as a basis for getting the discussion started.
3. Frame a clear, concise mandate statement, and regularly remind organizational members of what the organization is required to do. This ensures conformity with the mandates and identifies where the organization has discretionary authority and where it does not. (If mandates are an issue, they may need to be changed.)

WORKSHEET 7 Review of Mandates

Instructions: Use this worksheet as a guide, but create your own organizational mandate evaluation criteria.

Mandate	Source (Charter, Policy, Rules, Law, Norms, and so on)	Key Requirements	Effects on Organization	Evaluation Criteria
				☐ Funded ☐ Still appropriate ☐ Out-of-date ☐ Conflicts with others
				☐ Funded ☐ Still appropriate ☐ Out-of-date ☐ Conflicts with others
				☐ Funded ☐ Still appropriate ☐ Out-of-date ☐ Conflicts with others
				☐ Funded ☐ Still appropriate ☐ Out-of-date ☐ Conflicts with others
				☐ Funded ☐ Still appropriate ☐ Out-of-date ☐ Conflicts with others

WORKSHEET **8**   **Background for Group Discussion of Mandates**

Instructions: Individuals should first fill out this worksheet by themselves, as a basis for group discussion.

---

1. What is "mandated," and what are the types of mandates that we have? What does this mean about our purpose and nature as an organization? Which mandates can we change as an organization, and which ones require others (for example, the legislature or the courts) to be involved?

2. What impacts do these mandates have on our future direction as an organization, including their implications for resource availability and use?

3. What programs, services, and product areas, existing or potential, are *not* ruled out by mandates?

4. What is our organization's current mission in relation to its mandates? Is the mission consistent with the mandates, in conflict with them, unrelated to them, inappropriately linked with them, not taking full advantage of them, and so forth?

5. What mandates may need to be changed, eliminated, or added, and why?

Identify and Understand Stakeholders, Develop and Refine Mission and Values, and Consider Developing a Vision Sketch

■ Purpose of Step

The purpose of step 3 is to help planners understand more about the organization's stakeholders, develop and refine the organization's mission and values, and perhaps develop a vision statement to guide the rest of the process. The key to success for public and nonprofit organizations is satisfying important stakeholders according to each stakeholder's criteria for satisfaction. Mission, values, and vision should therefore be thought about in relation to those stakeholders.

Stakeholders

A stakeholder is any person, group, or organization that can place a claim on the organization's resources, attention, or output or is affected by its output. A stakeholder analysis is the means for identifying who the organization's internal and external stakeholders are, how they evaluate the organization, how they influence the organization, what the organization needs from them, and how important they are. A stakeholder analysis is particularly useful in providing valuable information about the political situation facing the organization.

The results of a stakeholder analysis can form the basis for the development and refinement of a mission statement, and they can also help determine who should be involved in the strategic planning process. (The readiness assessment and step 1 therefore involved some preliminary stakeholder analysis.) Whom you involve in this process and how you involve them will go a long way toward determining in practice whose process it is and how successful you are likely to be in implementing any plans that are developed. (Additional detailed advice on stakeholder analyses can be found in *Strategic Planning for Public and Nonprofit Organizations,* third edition (Bryson, 2004), especially Chapters Three and Four and Resource A.)

Mission

In step 3, the organization's mission is identified, developed, and refined—a process that may also include clarifying the organization's values.

A mission statement is an action-oriented formulation of the organization's reason for existence—its purpose. A mission statement answers the question, Ultimately, *what* are we here to do, and *why?* The mission statement should be developed in light of who the organization's stakeholders are and how the organization might create public value.

The mission statement for your organization should also define how the organization proposes to get from where it is to where it wants to go. The statement should be meaningful yet concise.

Values

Values underpin *how* the organization operates. If an organization wants to develop a values statement, the starting point should be the following questions: How do we want to conduct our business? How do we want to treat our key stakeholders? What do we value—in other words, what do we really care about? A statement of organizational values can be extremely helpful for understanding the organization's culture and the issues it faces and for developing organizational goals and strategies.

Vision

A vision statement—often called a *vision of success*—describes what the organization should look like as it successfully implements its strategies and achieves its full potential. An organization typically has to go through more than one cycle of strategic planning before it can develop an effective vision for itself. A vision of success is therefore more likely to be a guide to strategy implementation than to strategy formulation. That is why step 8 is explicitly devoted to developing a vision of success.

Nonetheless, many organizations find it very useful to develop a *vision sketch* in this step as a guide for the rest of the planning process and for the plan itself. The sketch is unlikely to be as detailed as a full-blown vision of success but still can be useful in directing participant attention in subsequent steps. For example, a vision sketch can be used to help planners identify strategic issues and formulate strategies to address the issues.

All that is really necessary to enhance organizational achievement is to identify a few key issues and to do something effective about them. Nonetheless, if the planning groups thinks it makes sense to develop a vision sketch, the group should do so.

■ Possible Desired Planning Outcomes

- An inclusive list of stakeholders and an analysis of how, where, when, and why to involve them in the process
- A draft mission statement
- A draft values statement
- A vision sketch

■ Worksheet Directions

Stakeholders

1. Have your strategic planning team brainstorm a list of key stakeholders (Worksheet 9) and fill out an analysis worksheet for each (Worksheets 10 and 11).
2. On the basis of this analysis, evaluate the involvement of stakeholders in the strategic planning process (Worksheets 12 and 13). If the planning effort is to be successful and if planned strategies are to be implemented, both the process and the plan need to involve and "speak to" key stakeholders. One important area of involvement for both internal and external stakeholders is development of the mission statement. Stakeholders may also need to be involved in development of the values statement and vision sketch.

Mission

1. Identify and organize any existing mission-related materials. Have the strategic planning team review the materials before filling out Worksheet 14.
2. Have one person or a small group prepare a draft mission statement. Circulate the draft to stakeholders for their comments. Expect to revisit the mission statement throughout the process.

Values

1. Consider developing an explicit statement of values that indicates how your organization wants to operate and relate to key stakeholders. Values such as respect, trust, honesty, integrity, and teamwork are often emphasized in such statements. The values statement should articulate a code of behavior to which the organization adheres or aspires.
2. Have the planning team collect any values-related material and review and discuss it. If there is none, consider developing it through group discussions with your team and key stakeholders. The values discussion can often identify strategic issues. Fill out Worksheet 15.
3. Have one person or a small group prepare a draft values statement and discuss it. Circulate drafts to key stakeholders for their comments. Expect to revisit the values statement throughout the process.

Vision

1. Have the planning team collect any vision-related materials and documents. Review and discuss these, then consider developing a vision sketch through group discussions with your team and key stakeholders. Think about the organization's mission and what its basic philosophy and values, strategies, and performance criteria are or should be. Think about how the organization would look if it were creating as much public value as possible.
2. Have the planning team members or key stakeholder representatives break into small groups and individually fill out Worksheet 16. The whole group should then share and discuss everyone's answers.
3. Following the discussion, request that someone or a small group prepare a draft vision sketch.
4. Circulate drafts to key stakeholders for their comments and make modifications as appropriate until general agreement is reached.
5. Communicate the organization's vision sketch to key stakeholders, both internal and external.
6. Expect to revisit the vision sketch throughout the process and especially in step 8. The sketch and any subsequent vision of success will change as the organization and the factors affecting the organization change.

WORKSHEET 9   Stakeholder Identification

Instructions: To begin a stakeholder analysis, list the organization's stakeholders. Be as inclusive as possible the first time around in filling out this worksheet. Later you and your group might consider deciding how important each stakeholder is in terms of positive or negative impact on the organization; its strategies; and its ability to fulfill its mission, meet its mandates, and create public value. A stakeholder analysis done early in the process can help you decide who should be involved in the process and when, how, and why. Additional stakeholder analyses are likely to be needed in the issues identification, strategy formulation, plan review and adoption, and implementation steps. Some stakeholders, like unions or policy board members, may be both internal and external stakeholders. Figure 6 on the next page is an example of how Worksheet 9 might be completed for a public agency.

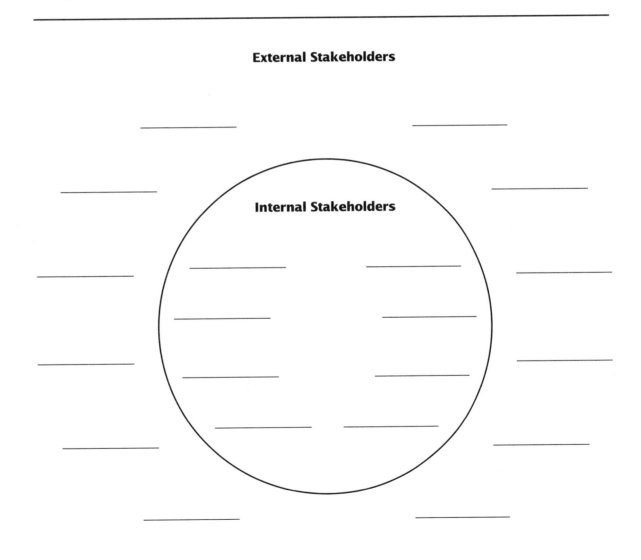

Figure 6 ■ Stakeholder Mapping Example for a Public Agency

WORKSHEET 10 External Stakeholder Analysis

Instructions: An external stakeholder is any person, group, or organization outside the organization that can make a claim on the organization's attention, resources, or output or that is affected by the organization's output. For example, an external stakeholder may be the organization's client or customer for goods and services, a service partner, a regulatory entity, a union, or taxpayers and the citizenry in general.

For each external stakeholder group listed on Worksheet 9, fill out a separate copy of this external stakeholder analysis worksheet. Rank your stakeholders in terms of their importance to your organization and their role.

Stakeholder's Name	Type of Stakeholder		
	Client or Customer	Partner	Other

Criteria Used by Stakeholder to Assess Our Performance	Our Sense of Their Judgment About Our Performance		
	Poor	Average	Good

1. How does this stakeholder affect us, and how do we affect this stakeholder?

2. What do we need from this stakeholder, and what does this stakeholder need from us?

3. How important is this stakeholder?

   ☐ Extremely

   ☐ Reasonably

   ☐ Not at all

4. What role should this stakeholder have in the strategic planning process, if any?

   ☐ Strategic planning coordinating committee member

   ☐ Strategic planning team member

   ☐ Participant in the process

   ☐ Plan reviewer

   ☐ Other

WORKSHEET 11   Internal Stakeholder Analysis

Instructions: An internal stakeholder is any person, group, or organization inside the organization that can make a claim on the organization's attention, resources, or output or that is affected by the organization's output. For example, internal stakeholders include board members, managers, and employees.

For each internal stakeholder group listed on Worksheet 9, fill out a separate internal stakeholder analysis worksheet. Rank your stakeholders in terms of their importance to your organization and their role.

Stakeholder's Name

Criteria Used by Stakeholder to Assess Our Performance	Our Sense of Their Judgment About Our Performance		
	Poor	Average	Good

1. How does this stakeholder affect us, and how do we affect this stakeholder?

2. What do we need from this stakeholder, and what does this stakeholder need from us?

3. How important is this stakeholder?

☐ Extremely

☐ Reasonably

☐ Not at all

4. What role should this stakeholder have in the strategic planning process, if any?

☐ Strategic planning coordinating committee member

☐ Strategic planning team member

☐ Participant in the process

☐ Plan reviewer

☐ Other

WORKSHEET 12 Key External Stakeholder Involvement

Instructions: Identifying the organization's stakeholders is an important early—and on-going—step in the strategic planning process. An organization's stakeholders include any person, group, or organization that can place a claim on the organization's attention, resources, or output or that is affected by that output.

Review Worksheets 9 and 10, and list the key external stakeholders that should be involved in the process. If they should, decide *how* they should be involved.

Key External Stakeholder's Name	Type of Involvement					
	Ignore	Inform	Consult	Collaborate or Involve	Decision Maker	Delegated Authority

After you have filled out the table, revisit the question of who needs to be engaged in the strategic planning process and how. Reconsider membership on the strategic planning co-ordinating committee, strategic planning team, and other relevant bodies. Think about how to engage key stakeholders in other ways, for example, through focus groups, discussion groups, surveys, or other methods.

The ideal size for a strategic planning team is probably four to seven people and certainly no more than nine. The team may be a subgroup of a larger group, such as the strategic planning coordinating committee, although that group should also not be too large. There is a trade-off between getting many people involved and still getting some action!

Having said that, we also advise being as inclusive as possible in engaging stakeholders in other ways. Good suggestions and new ideas will come into the process as a result, and the legitimacy of the process will be enhanced.

Keeping participants informed and appropriately engaged greatly increases ownership of the process, the plan, and its implementation. Developing an effective communication plan to keep participants informed of the strategic planning process and its progress is often very important for process and plan success.

WORKSHEET 13 Key Internal Stakeholder Involvement

Instructions: Identifying the organization's stakeholders is an important early—and on-going—step in the strategic planning process. An organization's stakeholders include any person, group, or organization that can place a claim on the organization's attention, resources, or output or that is affected by that output.

Review Worksheets 9 and 11, and list the key internal stakeholders in the following table. Then decide whether they should be involved in the process. If they should, decide *how* they should be involved.

Key Internal Stakeholder's Name	Type of Involvement					
	Ignore	Inform	Consult	Collaborate or Involve	Decision Maker	Delegated Authority

After you have filled out the table, revisit the question of who needs to be engaged in the strategic planning process and how. Reconsider membership on the strategic planning coordinating committee, strategic planning team, and other relevant bodies. Think about how to engage key stakeholders in other ways, for example, through focus groups, discussion groups, surveys, or other methods.

The ideal size for a strategic planning team is probably four to seven people and certainly no more than nine. The team may be a subgroup of a larger group, such as the strategic planning coordinating committee, although that group should also not be too large. There is a trade-off between getting many people involved and still getting some action!

Having said that, we also advise being as inclusive as possible in engaging stakeholders in other ways. Good suggestions and new ideas will come into the process as a result, and the legitimacy of the process will be enhanced.

Keeping participants informed and appropriately engaged greatly increases ownership of the process, the plan, and its implementation. Developing an effective communication plan to keep participants informed of the strategic planning process and its progress is often very important for process and plan success.

WORKSHEET 14 Mission Statement

Instructions: A mission statement should clarify the organization's purpose and indicate why it is doing what it does. In other words, it should answer the question, "Ultimately, what are we here to do?"

Individuals should fill out this worksheet first by themselves. After the whole group discusses the results, a single individual or small group may be charged with drafting a new mission statement for review by key stakeholders.

Do not be surprised if a strategic issue emerges from your discussion of your organization's mission statement.

1. What is our current mission? What does it say about who we are, what our purpose is, what business we are in, who we serve, and how we are unique?

2. In general, what are the basic social and political needs we exist to fill? Or, what are the basic social or political problems we exist to address?

3. What is our role in filling these needs or addressing these problems? How does it differ from the roles of other organizations?

4. In general, what do we want to do to recognize or anticipate and respond to these needs or problems?

5. How should we respond to our key stakeholders?

6. What is our philosophy, and what are our core values?

7. Is our current mission dated, and if so, how?

8. What changes in the mission would I propose?

9. Examine the answers to the prior questions and draft a mission statement.

   Example—The mission of the Los Angeles County Department of Children and Family Services: The Department of Children and Family Services will, with our community partners, provide a comprehensive child protection system of prevention, preservation, and permanency to ensure that children grow up safe, physically and emotionally healthy, educated, and in permanent homes.

WORKSHEET **15** **Values Statement**

Instructions: A values statement should articulate *how* the organization will conduct itself. The statement should answer the question, How do we want to treat others, and how do we want to be treated ourselves?

Do not be surprised if a strategic issue emerges from your discussion of your organization's value system.

We suggest that people work individually to answer the first three items and then complete the worksheet through group discussion.

---

1. List, in the following table, what you consider to be your organization's key values *in practice* at the present time. Note that an organization's values are most obvious in *how* it does things and *with whom* it does them, not in *what* it does. Note also that the *key* values may not be *good* values. (*Examples of desirable values:* honesty, integrity, caring, trust, and respect.)

Value	Is This a Desirable or Good Value?	Or Is This an Inappropriate or Bad Value?

2. List the additional values you would like to see your organization adopt to guide the conduct of its business and its relationships with key stakeholders.

3. Having identified both current values (desirable as well as inappropriate) and those you would like to see adopted, place an asterisk (*) next to the eight to ten values that you think are most important for the organization to embrace.

4. Engage in a group discussion, and develop working definitions for each of the five or six most important values on which most people can agree.

Value	Definition

5. Now consider how you want to reflect these top values in the strategic planning process and in the strategic plan (for example, as a values list, as broad statements, as criteria for selecting strategies, as part of your vision statement).

WORKSHEET 16 Vision Sketch

Instructions: A vision describes what the organization should look like as it successfully implements its strategies and achieves its full potential. A vision statement answers the question, Where and what do we want to be? That is, what might the organization look like or be in the future given expected opportunities, challenges, and completion of anticipated or conceivable actions?

Typically, an organization has to go through several cycles of strategic planning in order to develop a full-blown vision of success, which is one reason why vision development is step 8 in the Strategy Change Cycle. But often it makes sense to prepare a vision sketch earlier, as a way of giving direction to subsequent steps in the process—and this preliminary vision should be revisited and perhaps revised in those later steps.

Do not be surprised if a strategic issue (or more than one) emerges from your discussion of individuals' vision sketches.

We suggest that people work individually to answer the first three items and then complete the worksheet through group discussion.

---

1. Succinctly describe the organization as it is right now. Characterize its mission or role, people, services, structure, processes, resources, culture, and external legitimacy and support.

   ☐ Mission or role

   ☐ People

   ☐ Services

   ☐ Structure

   ☐ Processes

☐   Resources

☐   Culture

☐   External legitimacy and support

2. Now imagine it is five years in the future and you are a journalist reporting on your organization. What do you see in the following areas?

   ☐   Mission or role

   ☐   People

   ☐   Services

   ☐   Structure

   ☐   Processes

   ☐   Resources

☐   Culture

☐   External legitimacy and support

3. If your vision sketch for the organization is out of alignment with where you think things are at present, then indicate where the major misalignments or gaps are.

☐   Mission or role

☐   People

☐   Services

☐   Structure

☐   Processes

☐   Resources

☐   Culture

☐   External legitimacy and support

4. Engage in a group discussion in which you compare and contrast each other's vision sketches.

5. Assign an individual or small group the task of drafting a vision sketch that combines the best features of the individuals' sketches along with what appears to be the group's consensus views.

   Brief example—The guiding vision for the Los Angeles County Department of Children and Family Services: Children grow up safe, physically and emotionally healthy, educated, and in permanent homes.

6. Now consider how you want to use the vision sketch to guide the strategic planning process and how this vision will be reflected in the strategic plan (for example, to help identify strategic issues, to guide strategy selection, to guide implementation, to communicate with internal and external stakeholders).

Assess the Environment to Identify Strengths, Weaknesses, Opportunities, and Challenges

■ Purpose of Step

In step 4, the internal strengths and weaknesses of the organization are identified, along with the organization's external opportunities and challenges (or threats). The analysis of these four elements, known by the acronym SWOC, is very useful in clarifying the conditions or situations within which the organization operates. Whereas the stakeholder analysis (step 3) provides extraordinarily useful information about the politics impinging on the organization, the SWOC analysis supplies an overall systems view of the organization and the factors that affect it.

A SWOC analysis is a valuable prelude to identifying and framing strategic issues in step 5. People often want to jump straight to strategic issues without really understanding the context of the issues. As a result, strategic issues are often misidentified, which in turn means that the strategies developed in step 6 do not address the real issues. Solving the wrong problem is a classic mistake that a good SWOC analysis, in conjunction with a good stakeholder analysis, can help the organization avoid (Nutt, 2002). In addition, a SWOC analysis brings to the surface clues about the probable contours of effective strategies, because every successful strategy builds on strengths (and especially distinctive competencies, as described in the next paragraph) and takes advantage of opportunities while it also overcomes or minimizes the effects of weaknesses and challenges.

A SWOC analysis can help the organization identify its *critical success factors* (CSIs). These are the things the organization must do or criteria it must meet in order to be successful in the eyes of its key stakeholders, especially those in its external environment (Johnson and Scholes, 2002). *Competencies* are capabilities, sets of actions, or strategies at which the organization is particularly good, or the resources (broadly conceived) on which it can draw to perform well against its critical success factors. A *distinctive competency* is a competency that is difficult for others to replicate and so is a source of enduring organizational advantage (Eden and Ackermann, 1998; Ackermann, Eden, and Brown, 2004).

■ Possible Desired Planning Outcomes

- Lists of internal strengths and weaknesses and external opportunities and challenges
- Identification of the organization's competencies—a special kind of strength
- Key background reports
- Specific actions and ideas to build on strengths and take advantage of opportunities
- Specific actions and ideas to deal with challenges and weaknesses
- Thoughtful discussions among key decision makers concerning strengths, weaknesses, opportunities, and challenges and their implications

■ Worksheet Directions

1. Consider using the snow card technique (see Resource B) with the strategic planning team (SPT) to develop an initial list of internal strengths and weaknesses and external opportunities and challenges. Fill out Worksheets 17 through 21.
2. If possible, always have the SPT consider what is going on outside the organization before it considers what is going on inside.
3. When the SPT is reviewing its SWOC list, encourage team members to look for patterns, important actions that might be taken immediately, and implications for the identification of strategic issues.
4. Take the time, if at all possible, to clearly identify the organization's competencies and especially its distinctive competencies (Worksheet 21), because they are crucial to effective pursuit of any strategy.
5. To ensure accuracy and reasonable completeness, conduct a follow-up analysis of the SWOC list developed by the SPT.

WORKSHEET 17 Internal Strengths

Instructions: Internal strengths are resources or capabilities that help an organization accomplish its mandates or mission and create public value. (*Examples:* highly skilled staff, good morale, adequate resources, well-connected board, excellent information technology system, effective performance management system, effective communications system.)

1. Fill out as many worksheets as are necessary to derive a complete list of your organization's strengths. Put an asterisk (*) next to the eight to ten strengths you think are the most important. Discuss each of the high-priority strengths.
2. Identify any strategic issues that may be associated with the list.
3. Look at the list of options for preserving or enhancing strengths. Note with an asterisk (*) any that might be pursued immediately without unnecessarily or unwisely foreclosing future choices, then discuss.

Strength	Description	Options for Preserving or Enhancing Each Strength

WORKSHEET **18**   Internal Weaknesses

Instructions: Internal weaknesses are deficiencies in resources or capabilities that hinder an organization's ability to meet its mandates, fulfill its mission, and create public value. (*Examples:* poor internal and external communications, unclear mission or vision, structural misalignments, noncompetitive pay scales, low morale, inadequate resources.)

1. Fill out as many worksheets as are necessary to derive a complete list of your organization's weaknesses. Put an asterisk (*) next to the eight to ten weaknesses you think are the most important. Discuss each of the high-priority weaknesses.
2. Identify any strategic issues that may be associated with the list.
3. Look at the list of options for minimizing or overcoming the weaknesses. Note with an asterisk (*) any that might be pursued immediately without unnecessarily or unwisely foreclosing future choices, then discuss.

Weakness	Description	Options for Minimizing or Overcoming Each Weakness

WORKSHEET 19   External Opportunities

Instructions: External opportunities are outside factors or situations that the organization can take advantage of to better fulfill its mission, meet its mandates, or create public value. (*Examples:* new funding source, new potential service partner, chance to modify an outdated mandate, opportunity to pay off or refinance debt.)

1. Fill out as many worksheets as are necessary to derive a complete list of your organization's opportunities. Put an asterisk (*) next to the eight to ten opportunities you think are the most important. Discuss each of the high-priority opportunities.
2. Identify any strategic issues that may be associated with the list.
3. Look at the list of options for taking advantage of the opportunities. Note with an asterisk (*) any that might be pursued immediately without unnecessarily or unwisely foreclosing future choices, then discuss.

Opportunity	Description	Options for Taking Advantage of Each Opportunity

WORKSHEET **20**   **External Challenges**

Instructions: External challenges are outside factors or situations that can affect your organization in a negative way—making it harder for the organization to fulfill its mission, meet its mandates, or create public value. (*Examples:* loss of funding from an external source, new unfunded mandates, poor organizational image or reputation, poor union relations, lack of public support for key programs.)

1. Fill out as many worksheets as are necessary to derive a complete list of your organization's challenges. Put an asterisk (*) next to the eight to ten challenges you think are the most important. Discuss each of the high-priority challenges.
2. Identify any strategic issues that may be associated with the list.
3. Look at the list of options for overcoming the challenges. Note with an asterisk (*) any that might be pursued immediately without unnecessarily or unwisely foreclosing future choices, then discuss.

Challenge	Description	Options for Overcoming Each Challenge

WORKSHEET **21** Distinctive Competencies

Instructions: *Critical success factors* (CSFs) are the things the organization must do or the criteria it must meet in order to be successful in the eyes of its key stakeholders, especially those in the external environment. *Competencies* are capabilities, sets of actions, or strategies at which the organization is particularly good, or the resources (broadly conceived) on which it can draw to perform well against its critical success factors. A *distinctive competency* is a competency that is difficult for others to replicate and so is a source of enduring organizational advantage. A *core competency* is one central to the success of the organization. A *distinctive core competency* is not only central to the success of the organization but helps the organization add more public value than alternative providers do. (*Examples of distinctive core competencies:* ways of delivering services that are unique and especially valued by recipients, ways of maintaining the organization's reputation and stakeholders' trust in the organization that are far in excess of what rivals can do.)

1. Fill out the three columns in the following table. Use as many worksheets as you need.
2. Put an asterisk (*) next to competencies that are core competencies, then discuss.
3. Put a double asterisk (**) next to competencies that are distinctive core competencies, then discuss.

Critical Success Factors	Reasons the Organization Does Well Against the CSFs	Competencies— Capabilities or Resources— the Organization Can Draw On to Do Well Against the CSFs
Example: Services tailored to client needs	*Example:* Flexible client scheduling system	*Example:* Flexible, committed staff; excellent information management system, resources, and staff

STEP 5

Identify and Frame Strategic Issues

■ Purpose of Step

A *strategic issue* is a fundamental policy choice or *change challenge* affecting an organization's mandates, mission, product or service level and mix, clients or users, costs, financing, structure, processes, or management. The purpose of step 5 is to identify the set of strategic issues facing the organization and to frame them as questions or concerns the organization can do something about.

The identification of strategic issues is the heart of the strategic planning process.

The previous steps have been designed to provide several sources of information that will help you frame your organization's strategic issues in the most constructive way. The manner in which the issues are framed will determine much of the subsequent politics of the process. It will also have a powerful impact on how strategies are formulated, how stakeholders assess their interests and weigh costs and benefits of alternative strategies, and whether specific arguments are likely to be winners or losers in support of various strategies.

Issue framing will also directly affect the ease with which the plan can be implemented. When participants support the way the issues are framed, they are far more likely to commit to the strategies developed in the next step and to subsequent strategy implementation.

Many important issues are likely to have emerged before this step in the process. They will have emerged from planning the plan meetings; stakeholder analyses; mission, values, and vision discussions; environmental scans; and SWOC discussions. And an important issue or issues may have prompted the strategic planning effort in the first place. You should have been capturing and documenting these potential strategic issues all along.

Issues fall into three main categories:

- Current issues that probably require immediate action
- Issues that are likely to require action in the near future but can be handled as part of the organization's regular planning cycle
- Issues that require no action at present but need to be continuously monitored

Over the course of the Strategy Change Cycle generally—and in this step specifically—a number of issues are likely to emerge that are more *operational* or *tactical* than *strategic*. It is important to capture the operational issues, for three reasons. First, many participants will think that these operational issues are the ones that have the most impact on their day-to-day work and will want to see something done about them. Second, finding ways to take action on these operational issues often energizes the strategic planning process—because people see it leading to immediate results that directly affect their work lives, and they gain confidence that the organization is serious about dealing with strategic concerns as well. And third, addressing operational issues often simultaneously removes barriers to effectively confronting the organization's strategic issues. (*Example of the difference between strategic and operational issues:* When an organization realizes it is experiencing ineffective use of information technology, resulting in inefficient work flows, poor communication, poor client record keeping, and unacceptably low levels of client service and satisfaction, it has identified a *strategic issue.* When that organization realizes it has a lack of office connectivity and has not put enough desktop or laptop computers in the hands of the appropriate staff, it has identified an *operational issue.*)

It is often helpful to create an operations team (OT) to explore the operational and tactical issues and develop recommendations for action. Having an OT will allow the SPT and SPCC to stay focused on the strategic issues. As the SPT and SPCC identify operational and tactical issues—according to an agreed process and set of criteria—they will refer them to the OT for analysis, recommendations for action, and possible action. The OT might be a preexisting group of managers or else a small group composed of a cross-section of organizational employees.

■ Possible Desired Planning Outcomes

- An inclusive list of strategic and operational issues faced by the organization
- An ordering of the strategic issues in terms of priority, logic, sequence, or some other relevant classification

- Referral of operational issues to an operations team
- Creation of an OT if one does not already exist

■ Worksheet Directions

1. Have individual members of the strategic planning team fill out Worksheet 22, using one copy of the worksheet for each of five to nine possible issues identified.

2. Compare the individual responses given on Worksheet 22. Have the team members work together to fill out Worksheet 23, the master list of key strategic issues.

3. Have the strategic planning team develop a master strategic issue statement for each issue, using Worksheet 24.

4. Decide whether each issue is operational or strategic by applying the information in Worksheet 25. There is no absolute test to establish whether an issue is strategic or operational. Many issues will fall into a gray area, and the assessment of their strategic importance is a judgment that must be made by policymakers or top management. To assist leaders and managers in making this judgment, the questions in Worksheet 25 may be asked for each issue. Generally speaking, major strategic issues will be characterized by answers that fall predominantly in columns two and three of Worksheet 25. Operational issues will tend to be characterized by answers that fall predominantly in columns one and two.

5. Decide on priorities among issues on the master list (Worksheet 23). Consider using the dot technique for prioritizing. Start by placing the entire list of strategic issues on flipchart sheets. Then give each member of the strategic planning team five to seven colored stick-on dots, numbered in sequence from 1. He or she may "vote" for an issue by placing a dot next to it—*with the higher numbers reflecting higher priorities*. When everyone has thus indicated what he or she thinks are the most important strategic issues facing the organization, the weighted votes are tallied for each issue. The issues with the highest number of points then become the key strategic issues for consideration in the strategic planning process.

6. If necessary, develop a new master list of key strategic issues (Worksheet 23).

7. If necessary, develop new master strategic issue statements (Worksheet 24) for the key issues. Consider what your organization's goals might be in addressing each issue. Also remember that every strategic issue involves some form of conflict. Among the questions to be struggled over in the next step, strategy formulation, are the following:

What will be done?
How will it be done?
Where will it be done?
When will it be done?
Who will do it?
Who will benefit by it—and who will not?

WORKSHEET 22 Individual Strategic Issue Identification

Instructions: This worksheet allows you as an individual to start to identify the set of strategic issues that your organization faces. A *strategic issue* is a fundamental policy choice or change challenge affecting an organization's mandates, mission, product or service level and mix, clients or users, costs, financing, structure, processes, or management.

Complete a separate worksheet for each of five to nine issues.

1. What is the issue? Be sure to phrase the issue as a question the organization can do something about and that has more than one answer.

2. Why is this an issue? How is it related to the organization's SWOCs and to its ability to meets its mandates, fulfill its mission, realize its vision, or create public value?

Strengths	Weaknesses	Opportunities	Challenges (or Threats)

Mission	Mandates	Vision	Other

3. What are the consequences of not addressing this issue? What makes it a priority?

WORKSHEET 23 Master List of Key Strategic Issues

Instructions:

1. Prepare a master list of key issues phrased as questions that have more than one answer and that your organization can do something about.
2. After the list has been constructed, discuss the order in which issues should be listed (for example, order of overall importance, logical order, order in which they should be addressed).
3. Prepare a new version of the master list in which the issues are presented in the preferred order.

1.

2.

3.

4.

5.

6.

7.

8.

9.

_____

10.

_____

11.

_____

12.

_____

13.

_____

14.

_____

15.

_____

16.

WORKSHEET **24** **Master Strategic Issue Statement**

Instructions: The master list of key issues (Worksheet 23) identifies the major policy questions or change challenges that are the focus of the strategic planning effort. Fill out a separate issue statement worksheet for each issue on the master list of key issues.

1. What is the issue? Be sure to phrase the issue as a question that has more than one answer. The issue should be one the organization can do something about.

2. Why is this an issue? Why does the issue exist? How is it related to the organization's mission, mandates, vision (if one exists), internal and external strengths and weaknesses, or external opportunities and challenges (threats)?

   ☐ Mission

   ☐ Mandates

   ☐ Vision

   ☐ Strengths

☐   Weaknesses

☐   Opportunities

☐   Challenges (Threats)

3. What are the consequences of not addressing this issue?

4. What should our goals be in addressing this issue?

WORKSHEET 25   Operational Versus Strategic Issues

Issue:	The issue is: ☐ Primarily operational ☐ Primarily strategic		
	Operational ⟵		⟶ Strategic
1. Is the issue on the agenda of the organization's policy board (whether elected or appointed)?	No		Yes
2. Is the issue on the agenda of the organization's chief executive (whether elected or appointed)?	No		Yes
3. When will the strategic issue's challenge or opportunity confront you?	Right now	Next year	2 or more years from now
4. How broad an impact will the issue have?	Single unit or division		Entire organization
5. How large is your organization's financial risk or opportunity?	Minor (≤ 10% of budget)	Moderate (10–15% of budget)	Major (≥ 25% of budget)
6. Will strategies for issue resolution likely require:			
a. Change in mission?	No		Yes
b. Development of new service goals and programs?	No		Yes
c. Significant changes in revenue sources or amounts?	No		Yes
d. Significant amendments in federal or state statutes or regulations?	No		Yes
e. Significant staff changes?	No		Yes
f. Significant technology changes?	No		Yes
g. Major facility changes?	No		Yes
h. Major changes in stakeholder relationships?	No		Yes
7. How apparent is the best approach for issue resolution?	Obvious, ready to implement	Broad parameters, few details	Wide open
8. What is the lowest level of management that can decide how to deal with this issue?	Line staff supervisor		Head of major department
9. What are the probable consequences of not addressing this issue?	Inconvenience, inefficiency	Significant service disruption, financial losses	Major long-term service disruption and large cost or revenue setbacks
10. How many other groups are affected by this issue and must be involved in resolution?	None	1–3	4 or more
11. How sensitive or "charged" is this issue relative to community, social, political, religious, and cultural values?	Benign	Touchy	Dynamite

Formulate Strategies to Manage the Issues

■ Purpose of Step

The purpose of step 6 is to create a set of strategies to address each priority issue that has been identified in step 5, so that the organization can better fulfill its mission, meet its mandates, achieve its issue-specific goals, and in general create public value.

Strategy is a *pattern* of purposes, policies, programs, projects, actions, decisions, and resource allocations that defines what an organization is, what it does, and why it does it. Strategies can vary by level, function, and time frame.

■ Possible Desired Planning Outcomes

- Preparation of strategy statements of different kinds:
  Grand strategy for the organization as a whole
  Division or subunit strategy statements
  Program, service, product, project, or business process strategies
  Strategy statements for specific functions, such as human resource management, finance, and information technology
- Preparation of draft strategic plans
- Actions taken when they are identified and become useful or necessary

■ Worksheet Directions for Strategy Development

1. Remember that what is important is strategic thinking, acting, and learning, not a particular approach to strategy formulation or the development of a formal strategic plan. Step 6 is likely to be more

interactive than previous steps because of the need to find the best fit among strategies and the elements of each strategy.

2. Develop answers to the questions on Worksheet 26 (Spencer, 1989), which may be filled out by boards, the strategic planning team (SPT), task forces, operational managers and selected staff, or others. The same people do not have to answer all of the questions. The strategic planning coordinating committee or the SPT may tackle the first five, for example, and other work groups may be assigned the task of answering the next two. In some circumstances, answering the last two questions may be postponed until step 7 (review and adopt the strategic plan) has been completed.

3. Have the SPT organize the Worksheet 26 responses into coherent sets of strategies, showing how the strategies address particular issues or achieve issue-specific goals and identifying the parts of the organization that would be required to implement the strategies. Prepare a strategy statement for each strategy, using a copy of Worksheet 27 for each one.

4. Make sure that strategies are described in reasonable detail, to allow people to make informed judgments about their efficacy and to provide reasonable guidance for assessing the implications for implementation and for the organization in general.

5. Ask the SPT to establish criteria for the evaluation of each suggested strategy. The team may use Worksheet 28, filling out one copy for each strategy.

6. Allow for consultation between the SPT and key stakeholders, so that the planning team can determine priorities among strategies for each issue or issue-related goal.

7. Develop a final strategy statement for each strategy, using the responses to Worksheets 26, 27, and 28 as a guide.

8. Encourage the SPT to develop a draft strategic plan. Information may be drawn from prior worksheets, and the checklist in Worksheet 29 may be used for deciding what should go in the plan.

■ Worksheet Directions for Plan Development

1. Prepare a draft strategic plan. Use the checklist in Worksheet 29 to decide what should go in the plan.
2. Even if you do not prepare a formal strategic plan, consider developing a set of interrelated strategy statements describing
    The grand strategy
    Organizational subunit strategies
    Program, service, product, project, or business strategies
    Functional strategies

3. Employ a structured process to review strategy statements and formal strategic plans. Review sessions may be structured around the following agenda:

   Overview of plan

   General discussion of plan and reactions to it

   Brainstorming a list of the strengths and weaknesses of the plan

   Brainstorming a list of the opportunities and challenges (threats) presented by the plan

   Brainstorming a list of modifications to improve on strengths and opportunities and minimize or overcome weaknesses and challenges (threats)

   Agreement on next steps to complete the plan

WORKSHEET **26** Key Questions for Identifying Strategies

Instructions: Fill out a separate worksheet for each key strategic issue. Be open to all ideas and build on the ideas of others. Challenge ideas (and the issue) in a constructive and positive way. Take the time to fully explore possible strategies.

1. The strategic issue is:

   (*Example:* How can we improve internal communications across and up and down our organization?)

2. Our issue-specific goals (or desired outcomes) are (or should be):

   (*Examples:* effective two-way communications, real-time feedback on organizational operations, improved collaboration.)

3. What are some practical alternatives, dreams, or visions we might pursue to address this issue and achieve our goal(s) or outcome(s)?

   (*Examples:* establish appropriate forums for communications; improve use of technology, newsletters, and other media; establish personnel performance evaluation criteria around communications responsibilities; lead by example.)

4. What are the possible barriers to our realizing these strategy alternatives?

   (*Examples:* management resistance, poorly designed organizational structure, distance between offices.)

5. What major initiatives might we pursue to achieve these alternatives, dreams, or visions directly or to achieve them indirectly through overcoming the barriers?

   (*Examples:* commission study of organizational communications, top management commitment to series of monthly town meetings, periodic survey of stakeholders to assess their communication needs.)

6. What are the key actions (with existing resources of people and dollars) that must be taken this year to implement the major initiatives?

   (*Examples:* establish performance reporting and accountability expectations around communication; design and commission study of organizational communication.)

7. What specific steps could be taken in the next six months to implement the major initiatives, and who would be responsible for taking them?

Step	Party Responsible
Example: Develop organizational communication project plan	Senior management
Example: Explore technology solutions to improve communications	IT director

WORKSHEET **27** **Strategy Statement**

Instructions: Fill out a separate strategy statement worksheet for each strategy.

1. What is the purpose of the strategy?

2. What are the goals (or desired outcomes) of the strategy?

3. How does the strategy address the issue and achieve the issue-specific goals?

4. What parts of the organization are required to implement the strategy?

   ☐ Whole organization

   ☐ Department(s)

   ☐ Division(s)

   ☐ Unit(s)/function(s)

5. Which stakeholders and aspects of stakeholder relationships are crucial for effective implementation of the strategy?

Stakeholder	Crucial Aspects of Relationship

WORKSHEET 28 Criteria for Evaluating Suggested Strategies

Instructions: Identify the specific strategy to be evaluated and critique it against the criteria you have developed. Be sure to take the time to discuss and agree on the criteria to be used to evaluate the appropriateness of specific strategies. Do not overdo the number or strictness of criteria to the point that you are not able to exercise judgment and make wise choices.

1. The issue the strategy is meant to address:

2. The proposed strategy:

3. Goals the strategy is meant to achieve:

4. Objectives:

5. Criteria used to evaluate strategies:

   Examples:
   - Acceptability to key decision makers, stakeholders, and opinion leaders
   - Acceptability to the general public
   - Client or user impact
   - Relevance to addressing the issue
   - Consistency with vision, mission, values, philosophy, and culture
   - Coordination or integration with other strategies, programs, and activities
   - Technical feasibility
   - Budget impacts, cost, and financing
   - Assured resources
   - Cost effectiveness
   - Return on investment
   - Long-term impacts
   - Short-term impacts
   - Risk assessment
   - Staff requirements
   - Flexibility or adaptability
   - Timing
   - Facility requirements

Other appropriate criteria:

WORKSHEET **29** Checklist for Deciding on Strategic Plan
Contents

Instructions: Strategic plans vary in their content and design. The same organization may use different plan formats for different purposes—for example, an executive summary for general distribution and a detailed plan for staff. The following elements might be included, but not necessarily in the order shown here.

Element	See Worksheet(s)	Include Yes	Include No
☐ Executive summary			
☐ Introduction	6		
☐ Purpose	6		
☐ Process	6		
☐ Stakeholder participation	12, 13		
☐ Mission statement	14		
☐ Values statement	15		
☐ Vision statement	16, 32		
☐ Mandates	7, 8		
☐ Environmental analysis, including SWOCs	17, 18, 19, 20, 21		
☐ Strategic issues	23, 24		
☐ Goals, objectives, and outcomes	10, 11, 14, 15, 24, 27, 35		
☐ Grand strategy statement	26, 27		
☐ Issue-specific strategy statements	23, 24, 26		
☐ Subunit strategy statements	26, 27		
☐ Implementation and action plans	26, 27, 33, 34, 35, 36		
☐ Other related plans			
☐ Human resources	26, 27, 33, 34, 35, 36		
☐ Information technology	26, 27, 33, 34, 35, 36		
☐ Financial	26, 27, 33, 34, 35, 36		
☐ Communications	26, 27, 33, 34, 35, 36		
☐ Marketing	26, 27, 33, 34, 35, 36		
☐ Other	26, 27, 33, 34, 35, 36		
☐ Monitoring and evaluation plans	37, 38		
☐ Plan for updating the plan	37, 38		

STEP 7

Review and Adopt the Strategic Plan

■ Purpose of Step

The purpose of step 7 is to reach an official organizational decision to adopt and proceed with the strategic plan or plans. This step may merge with step 6 (formulate strategies to manage the issues and prepare a draft strategic plan) in a single organization. But a separate step is likely to be necessary when strategic planning is undertaken for a large organization or for a community or a network of organizations. In the latter two cases the strategic planning coordinating committee (SPCC) will need to adopt the plan, and implementing organizations will also need to adopt it—or at least parts of it—in order for implementation to proceed effectively.

Step 7 generally marks the transition from strategic *planning* to strategic *management*.

■ Possible Desired Planning Outcomes

- Widely shared agreement on the strategic plan among key decision makers, and a decision to adopt the plan and proceed with implementation.
- Provision of the necessary guidance and resources for implementation. (It is important that the funding necessary to implement the plan be identified and allocated. Nothing is more disruptive to effective implementation and to the credibility of the planning effort than to have no resources for implementation.)
- Substantial support from internal and external stakeholders who can strongly affect implementation success.
- Widely shared sense of excitement about the substance and symbolism of the plan and the process.

■ Worksheet Directions

1. Determine who needs to be involved in reviewing and adopting the strategic plan (Worksheet 30).

    Continue to pay attention to the goals, concerns, and interests of all key stakeholders.

    Obtain necessary resource commitments, if at all possible, prior to the formal adoption session.

    Remember that incentives must reward behavior that will lead to effective implementation.

    Assess the nature and strength of supporting and opposing coalitions.

    Build support for the plan.

    Identify one or more sponsors and champions to gain passage in the relevant arenas.

2. Have your team assess how best to reach key stakeholders.

    Reduce decision-maker uncertainty about the proposed plan.

    Develop arguments and counterarguments in support of the proposal prior to formal review sessions.

    Engage formal review bodies in structured review sessions that focus on proposal strengths, (perhaps) weaknesses, and modifications that would improve strategies (Worksheet 31).

    Remember that some people or groups may not want the plan to be adopted or implemented under any circumstances.

3. Appoint a lead person (writer) or small team to produce the actual plan (if one has not already been prepared) and obtain the necessary reviews.

    Line up graphic and printing support early in the process. Content is the substance of the plan; graphics provide the style. You need both in an appropriate design to make the plan an effective communication vehicle. Great ideas badly presented can lose their greatness.

    Be prepared to bargain and negotiate over proposal features or other issues in exchange for support. This is part of the process.

    As part of ongoing communications efforts, provide public announcements of the plan's progress, at least within the organization and for key stakeholders.

WORKSHEET 30 Plan Review and Adoption Process

Instructions: Have a small team from the organization conduct an initial review of the draft plan to catch any glaring problems. Consider using this group to lead the more formal review process, including communicating the contents of the draft plan and getting stakeholder feedback. Be inclusive in your plan review process.

1. Determine who needs to participate in reviewing and adopting the plan in order to achieve the maximum plan ownership. (Be inclusive.)

Plan review	Plan Adoption

2. Review your stakeholder lists and assess who will likely support or oppose the plan or key plan elements and what their "issue" is and why.

Support	Opposition

3. Discuss what can be done to maintain plan support and to convert opposition to support.

4. Develop and communicate a plan review and adoption process.

What Will Be Done	Who Will Do It	When Will It Be Done	How Will It Be Done

5. Outline a communications and information process to inform stakeholders of the plan, the review process, and its adoption. (*Examples:* all staff meetings, memos, newsletters, meetings, focus groups.)

6. Make sure *key* resources necessary for implementation are identified and indicate whether or not they are assured. Do not forget personnel, information technology, and communication resources.

Resource	Assured	
	Yes	No

WORKSHEET **31**   **Plan Evaluation**

Instructions: List the strengths, weaknesses, and modifications that would improve the plan. If time is short, skip the weaknesses and concentrate on strengths and modifications that will improve on the strengths.

1. Strengths of the strategic plan:

2. Weaknesses of the strategic plan:

3. Modifications that will improve the strategic plan:

STEP 8

Establish an Effective Organizational Vision for the Future

■ Purpose of Step

In step 8, an organizational *vision of success* is prepared, describing what the organization should look like as it successfully implements its strategies, fulfills its mission, meets its mandates, creates public value, and in general achieves its full potential. An organization typically has to go through more than one cycle of strategic planning before it can develop a truly effective vision for itself. A vision of success is therefore more likely to be a guide to strategy implementation than to strategy formulation.

All that is absolutely necessary to enhance organizational achievement is to identify a few key issues and do something effective about them. Nonetheless, if a vision of success can be prepared, it should be. Indeed a number of organizations will have prepared at least a sketch of a vision of organizational success in step 3 and will then have used that sketch to guide subsequent steps in the process. A full-blown vision of success can be extremely important for educational purposes and for allowing people anywhere in the organization to take constructive action without constant oversight by leaders and managers.

■ Possible Desired Planning Outcomes

- Preparation of a short and inspiring vision of success
- Wide circulation of the vision among organizational members and other key stakeholders after appropriate consultations, reviews, and sign-offs
- Use of the vision to influence major and minor organizational decisions and actions

■ Worksheet Directions

1. Review the responses to Worksheet 16, if it has been used.
2. Have your team collect the available vision-related materials and documents. Review and discuss them, then consider developing a vision statement through individual work and group discussions with your team and key stakeholders. Many of the elements of a vision of success will have been described in the course of the strategic planning process. A vision of success should include the following information about the organization:

   Mission
   Basic philosophy and core values
   Basic strategies
   Performance criteria
   Major decision rules
   Ethical standards applied to all employees

3. Have your team members or key stakeholder representatives break into small groups. First, each individual fills out Worksheet 32. Then the members of each small group share and discuss their answers, and finally the larger group discusses the results.
4. Following the discussion, request that someone prepare a draft vision statement.
5. Circulate the draft to key stakeholders for their comments, and make modifications as appropriate until general agreement is reached.
6. Communicate your organization's vision statement to key stakeholders, both internal and external.
7. Expect to revisit the vision statement throughout the implementation process and in the future. The vision will change as the organization and the factors affecting the organization change.

WORKSHEET 32   Vision of Success

Instructions: Fill out the worksheet first, working individually, and then discuss with others.

---

1. What is the organization's mission? (See Worksheet 14.) Articulate the public value that the organization does or should create.

2. What are the organization's basic philosophies and core values? (See Worksheet 15.)

3. What are its basic strategies? (See Worksheet 27.)

4. What are the organization's performance criteria? (See Worksheets 7, 8, 10, 11, 14, 15, 24, 26, 27, and 28.)

5. What are the major decision rules followed by the organization?

   ■ What processes and procedures are followed to make major decisions?

   ■ What is decided centrally?

   ■ What is delegated?

   ■ How are exceptions handled?

6. What are the ethical standards expected of all employees?

7. Draft a vision statement for your organization, based on your answers to the first six questions.

Develop an Effective Implementation Process

■ Purpose of Step

The purpose of step 9 is to incorporate adopted strategies throughout the relevant organizational systems. The mere creation of a strategic plan is not enough. Developing an effective action plan and implementation process and providing the necessary resources will bring life to the strategies and create real value for the organization and its stakeholders.

Adequate funding and other resources are required for successful implementation. It does not matter how great the strategies and plan are if there is no capacity to carry them forward. However, not all strategies require "new" money. Many may be implemented by shifting existing organizational resources around. If the organization is unwilling to shift resources to match its priorities, then it probably should not have undertaken strategic planning in the first place.

■ Possible Desired Planning Outcomes

- Added public value through goal achievement and heightened stakeholder satisfaction
- Clear understanding of what needs to be done, by whom, when, where, how, and why
- Reasonably smooth and rapid introduction of the strategies throughout the relevant systems; adoption of the changes by all relevant organizations, units, groups, and individuals in a timely fashion
- Development of a widely shared vision of success to guide implementation (if one was not developed earlier)
- Use of a *debugging* process to identify and fix difficulties that almost inevitably arise as a new strategy is put into place

- Use of a formal evaluation process to determine whether substantive and symbolic strategic goals have been achieved
- Assurance that important features of the strategy are maintained throughout the implementation process
- Establishment of or provision for review points at which maintenance, replacement, or termination of the strategies can be considered
- Timely updating of the strategic plan and relevant implementation plans

■ Worksheet Directions

1. Think strategically about implementation. Consciously manage implementation so that important public and nonprofit purposes are furthered and public value is created.
2. Clearly document your organization's existing programs, services, and projects, using Worksheet 33. An understanding of what the organization is currently doing is the starting point for the effective integration of the strategic planning priorities. The organization will need to shift some or all of its efforts and resources to the higher-level priorities reflected in the strategic plan.
3. Using Worksheet 34, document the strategic plan's program, service, and project impacts. Then use Worksheet 35 to reconcile the organization's current activities with those envisioned in the strategic plan.
4. For each strategy developed through the strategic planning process, develop a clearly defined action plan (Worksheet 36) that answers the who, what, how, where, and when questions. Involve the operational and administrative stakeholders in this key step. (The organization's resource situation and mandates may make a phased approach to the implementation of the strategic plan necessary.) Action plans, which must be carefully coordinated, should detail
    Specific expected results, objectives, and milestones
    Roles and responsibilities of implementation bodies, teams, and individuals
    Specific action steps
    Schedules
    Resource requirements and sources
    A communication process
    A review and monitoring process
    Accountability processes and procedures
5. If necessary for effective follow-through, replace the strategic planning team with an implementation planning team, whose membership may be different although some overlap in membership is typically highly desirable.

WORKSHEET 33 Existing Programs, Services, and Projects: Evaluation

Existing Programs, Services, Projects	Criteria for Establishing Priority	Priority (Low/ Moderate/ High)	Client, Stakeholder, and Organizational Impact	Resources Used		Time Frame
				People	$	

WORKSHEET 34   Strategic Plan's Proposed Programs, Services, and Projects: Evaluation

Proposed Programs, Services, Projects	Criteria for Establishing Priority	Priority (Low/ Moderate/ High)	Client, Stakeholder, and Organizational Impact	Resources Used		Time Frame
				People	$	

WORKSHEET **35** Prioritizing Programs, Services, and Projects

Instructions: Using Worksheets 33 and 34, compile a master list of priorities that reconciles the organization's current programs, services, and projects with those proposed in the strategic plan.

Existing Priorities That Should Be Retained (Programs, Services, Projects)	Strategic Plan Priorities That Should Be Pursued (Programs, Services, Projects)

WORKSHEET 36 Action Planning

Instructions: For each priority listed on Worksheet 35, explore the following aspects of an action plan.

---

1. The priority is:

2. The relevant strategy is:

3. What specific actions must be taken to implement the strategy in the next six months to a year?

4. What are the expected results and milestones?

5. Who are the responsible parties? What are their roles and responsibilities?

6. When and where will the actions be taken?

7. What resources will be required, and where will they be obtained?

8. What communication process will be followed?

9. How will action plan implementation be reviewed and monitored and accountability ensured?

Reassess Strategies and the Strategic Planning Process

■ Purpose of Step

The purpose of this final step is to review implemented strategies and the strategic planning process as a prelude to a new cycle of strategic planning. Much of the work of this phase may have occurred as part of the ongoing implementation process. However, if an organization has not engaged in strategic planning for a while, it may be useful to mark off this step as a separate one.

In this step you need to reassess strategies—and the strategic issues that prompted them—in order to decide what should be done about them. Strategies may need to be maintained, superseded by other strategies, or terminated for one reason or another.

An attempt is also made in this step to figure out whether a new round of strategic planning is warranted and, if so, at what level and when. In doing this review, figure out how to build on the success you have had in implementation and the lessons learned. Strategic planning should build on past efforts. As organizational capacity for strategic thinking, acting, and learning increases, the strategic planning process should become easier.

■ Possible Desired Planning Outcomes

- Assurance that implemented strategies remain responsive to real needs and problems—and if they don't, consideration of what should be done with them
- Resolution of residual problems that become evident during sustained implementation

- Clarification of the strengths and weaknesses of the most recent strategic planning effort, and discussion of modifications that might be made in the next round of strategic planning
- Development of the energy, will, and ideas necessary to revise existing strategies, address important unresolved strategic issues, or undertake a full-blown strategic planning exercise

■ Worksheet Directions

1. At some point after implementation of the strategic plan has begun, evaluate not only the plan but the strategic planning process itself.

2. Strategy implementation is an ongoing process, not a one-time event, and the most effective way to improve it is to evaluate the success of prior efforts. Consider who should be involved in this evaluation effort (for example, key stakeholders, outside experts, strategic planning team, implementers). (Use Worksheet 37.)

3. On the basis of the evaluation and its findings, decide whether a new round of strategic plans is needed and what changes might be indicated. If a new round is thought necessary, fill out Worksheet 38 as a first step in charting possible improvements.

WORKSHEET 37 Improving Existing Strategies

Strategy	Strengths	Weaknesses	Modifications That Would Improve	Summary Evaluation
				☐ Maintain ☐ Replace with a new or revised element ☐ Terminate
				☐ Maintain ☐ Replace with a new or revised element ☐ Terminate
				☐ Maintain ☐ Replace with a new or revised element ☐ Terminate
				☐ Maintain ☐ Replace with a new or revised element ☐ Terminate
				☐ Maintain ☐ Replace with a new or revised element ☐ Terminate
				☐ Maintain ☐ Replace with a new or revised element ☐ Terminate

Planning Process Element	Strengths	Weaknesses	Modifications That Would Improve	Summary Evaluation
				☐ Maintain ☐ Replace with a new or revised element ☐ Terminate
				☐ Maintain ☐ Replace with a new or revised element ☐ Terminate
				☐ Maintain ☐ Replace with a new or revised element ☐ Terminate
				☐ Maintain ☐ Replace with a new or revised element ☐ Terminate
				☐ Maintain ☐ Replace with a new or revised element ☐ Terminate
				☐ Maintain ☐ Replace with a new or revised element ☐ Terminate

Resources

A. Brainstorming Guidelines

1. Agree to participate in a brainstorming exercise.

2. Do not criticize or evaluate any of the ideas that are put forward; they are simply placed before the group and recorded.

3. Be open to hearing some wild ideas in the spontaneity that evolves when the group suspends judgment. Practical considerations are not important at this point. The session is meant to be freewheeling.

4. Emphasize that the quantity of ideas counts, not their quality. All ideas should be expressed, and none should be screened out by any participant. A great number of ideas will increase the likelihood of the group's discovering good ones.

5. Build on the ideas of other group members when possible. Pool your creativity. Everyone should be free to build onto ideas and to make interesting amalgams from the various suggestions.

6. Focus on a *single* problem or issue. Don't skip around to various problems or try to brainstorm answers to multiple, complex problems.

7. Foster a congenial, relaxed, cooperative atmosphere.

8. Make sure that *all* members, no matter how shy and reluctant to contribute, get their ideas heard.

9. Record all ideas.

B. Snow Card Guidelines

1. Bring a single problem or issue into the group.

2. Have individuals in the group brainstorm as many ideas as possible and record them on individual worksheets.

3. Ask individuals to pick out their five "best items" and to transcribe each one onto its own *snow card*—half of an 8 1/2-by-11-inch sheet of paper, a 5-by-7-inch card, or a large Post-It note.

4. Shuffle the cards. Then tape them to a wall, in categories. The group should determine the categories after reviewing several of the items. The resulting clusters of cards may suggest a "blizzard" of ideas—hence the term *snow card*.

5. Establish subcategories as needed.

6. Once all items are on the wall and included in a category, rearrange and tinker with the categories until they make the most sense.

7. When finished, take down the cards, category by category, and have all the ideas typed up and distributed to the group. Alternatively, have someone enter the results on a laptop computer before the snow cards are taken down.

Source: These guidelines are based on a technique developed by Richard B. Duke of the University of Michigan and by the Institute of Cultural Affairs (Spencer, 1989).

C. Strategic Planning Workshop Equipment Checklist

- ☐ Strategic planning process outlines
- ☐ Strategic planning workbooks (*Creating and Implementing Your Strategic Plan, second edition*)
- ☐ Strategic planning books (Bryson, 2004)
- ☐ Strategic planning videos
- ☐ Sample strategic plans
- ☐ Snow cards (35 per person) (see Resource B)
- ☐ Broad-tipped marking pens for snow cards (dark colors)
- ☐ Flipcharts and easels (two or more)
- ☐ Broad-tipped marking pens for flipcharts or whiteboards (various colors)
- ☐ Masking tape
- ☐ Drafting tape
- ☐ Stick-on dots in different colors
- ☐ Post-it notes
- ☐ Overhead projector (including spare bulb)
- ☐ Blank transparencies
- ☐ Nonpermanent marking pens for transparencies
- ☐ Screen
- ☐ Video monitor
- ☐ VCR
- ☐ Laptop computer and printer
- ☐ LCD projector
- ☐ Audiocassette player
- ☐ Extension cords and power strips
- ☐ Digital camera (or still camera, film, and flash attachment) and access to one-hour photo processing
- ☐ Access to photocopy machine
- ☐ Secretarial support

D. Conference Room Setup Checklist

- ☐ Good lighting and ventilation
- ☐ Comfortable setting, free of distractions and phones
- ☐ Small tables that can be moved out of the way
- ☐ Comfortable, movable chairs
- ☐ Adequate breakout area(s)
- ☐ Walls to which flipcharts or snow cards can be taped
- ☐ Adequate electrical outlets
- ☐ Extension cords and power strips
- ☐ Coffee, tea, soft drinks, mineral water
- ☐ Bread, rolls
- ☐ Fresh fruit
- ☐ Hard candies
- ☐ Adequate restroom facilities

E. Model External Stakeholder (or Customer) Questionnaire for XYZ Organization

This questionnaire, for the fictitious XYZ Organization, is presented as a model only. A questionnaire of this type must be tailored to fit the organization in which it is to be administered. Every organization must choose its own best approach when conducting an external assessment.

Date:

To: XYZ Organization Stakeholders [or "Customers"]

From: Executive Director of XYZ Organization

First, I would like to thank all of you in advance for taking the time and effort to review and complete the attached customer service questionnaire.

A few years ago, XYZ developed a strategic plan to

- Update our mission, vision, and value statements and our goals, objectives, and strategies for accomplishing our mission of providing services that are high quality, on time, fiscally responsible, and convenient for our stakeholders [or "customers"]—you, the organizations that we serve
- Develop an action plan and timetable to implement our strategies
- Develop performance indicators and a process for measuring customer service and organizational effectiveness and efficiency
- Establish a process and key milestones to be used by XYZ management in monitoring implementation of the strategic plan

This questionnaire is a follow-up opportunity for you to provide our organization with some feedback on implementation of our strategies. It is another chance to raise customer service improvement issues and suggestions. All ideas will be considered.

If you have any questions about completing the questionnaire, please contact [name and contact information].

The ABC Company (whom we have hired to conduct this survey) will keep all questionnaires confidential and the results will be compiled in a manner that does not disclose individual responses.

If possible, please complete the questionnaire electronically, as this will speed the process of tabulating the information. Please e-mail the completed questionnaire, as an attachment, to the ABC Company, at [e-mail address], or mail to the ABC Company at [mailing address].

Please return your responses by [date].
Thank you again for your participation.

EXTERNAL CUSTOMER QUESTIONNAIRE

Please complete the following information:

My organization is: _____

My program area is: _____

Instructions for Completion

There are no "right" or "wrong" answers.

1. For each question in this questionnaire please *circle* the number from 1 to 10 that most closely reflects how you feel about the set of statements in that question.

2. If a set of statements does not apply to your position in the organization, please mark the NA (not applicable) blank.

Please be candid in your responses, and draw on your most recent experiences in the last two years.

Sample Question

Resources

1	2	3	4	5	6	7	(8)	9	10	NA ____

Resources are likely
to increase in the next
five years.

Resources are not likely
to increase in the next
five years.

Circling 1 would indicate a strong agreement with the left-hand statement ("Resources are likely to increase in the next five years").

Circling 10 would indicate strong agreement with the right-hand statement ("Resources are not likely to increase in the next five years").

Circling 8 would indicate moderate agreement with the right-hand statement, and so forth.

If you have any questions please contact Dr. Jane Smith of The ABC Company at [phone number or e-mail address].

I. USE OF XYZ ORGANIZATION'S SERVICES

A. Use of XYZ Services

Please indicate the XYZ services used by your organization. Mark the NA blank for XYZ services not used by your organization. [Add questions to this "use" section to cover each major service.]

Use of XYZ's XXX Service

1	2	3	4	5	6	7	8	9	10	NA _____

Our organization is a
relatively small user
of XYZ's XXX service.

Our organization is a
relatively large user
of XYZ's XXX service.

B. Timeliness of XYZ Services Used by Your Organization

Please rate the timeliness of XYZ services used by your organization. Mark the NA blank for XYZ services not used by your organization. [Add questions to this "timeliness" section to cover each major service.]

Timeliness of XYZ's XXX Service

1	2	3	4	5	6	7	8	9	10	NA _____

XYZ's XXX service is not
very timely.

XYZ's XXX service is
very timely.

C. Quality of XYZ Services Used by Your Organization

Please rate the quality of XYZ services used by your organization. Mark the NA blank for XYZ services not used by your organization. [Add questions to this "quality" section to cover each major service.]

Quality of XYZ's XXX Service

1	2	3	4	5	6	7	8	9	10	NA _____

The quality of XYZ's XXX
service needs improvement.

The quality of XYZ's XXX
service is excellent.

D. Cost of XYZ Services Used by Your Organization

Please rate the cost of XYZ services used by your organization. Mark the NA blank for XYZ services not used by your organization. [Add questions to this "cost" section to cover each major service.]

Cost of XYZ's XXX Service

1	2	3	4	5	6	7	8	9	10	NA _____

The cost of XYZ's XXX
service is appropriate.

The cost of XYZ's XXX
service is too high.

Comments

Please use the following space to comment on your organization's use of XYZ services.

You may include items not specifically addressed in the survey questions or expand on your responses to particular survey items. Please feel free to comment on why your organization does or does not use certain XYZ services. Also feel free to suggest other services that you would like to see XYZ provide to your organization.

If you prefer, you may write out your comments in a separate file, titled "Comments," or on separate pieces of paper. Be sure to attach this separate file to your e-mail or mail the papers with the questionnaire when it is returned.

II. GENERAL OBSERVATIONS ABOUT XYZ ORGANIZATION

1. Mission and Vision

   1   2   3   4   5   6   7   8   9   10   NA _____

   XYZ's mission and vision.   XYZ's mission and vision
   are relevant and clear.   are outdated or unclear.

2. Service Versus Procedural Compliance

   1   2   3   4   5   6   7   8   9   10   NA _____

   XYZ seems guided by its   In its daily activities, XYZ
   mission and vision   seems oriented toward
                                                      day-to-day procedures.

3. Knowledge of Stakeholders [or "Customers"]

   1   2   3   4   5   6   7   8   9   10   NA _____

   XYZ understands us   XYZ does not have a clear
   and our needs.   understanding of our
                                                      organization or our business.

4. Environmental Scanning

   1   2   3   4   5   6   7   8   9   10   NA _____

   XYZ seems to routinely   XYZ does not seem to
   monitor changes in its   routinely monitor changes
   work environment.   in its work environment.

5. Change

   1   2   3   4   5   6   7   8   9   10   NA _____

   Overall XYZ seems to see   Overall XYZ tends to avoid
   change as an opportunity.   change or to view it as high risk.

6. Information Technology

   1   2   3   4   5   6   7   8   9   10   NA _____

   XYZ uses technology   XYZ makes ineffective
   effectively in its   use of technology in its
   organizational management.   organizational management.

7. Definition of Decision-Making Processes

   1   2   3   4   5   6   7   8   9   10   NA _____

   XYZ's decision-making   XYZ's decision-making
   processes are poorly defined.   processes are clearly defined.

8. Adherence to Decision-Making Processes

1	2	3	4	5	6	7	8	9	10	NA _____

Decision-making processes seem inconsistently followed in XYZ.

Decision-making processes seem consistently followed in XYZ.

9. Information

1	2	3	4	5	6	7	8	9	10	NA _____

In XYZ, information seems to be viewed as a resource and is generally shared.

In XYZ, information seems to be used as a basis for power and is generally tightly controlled.

10. Synergy

1	2	3	4	5	6	7	8	9	10	NA _____

People in XYZ seem willing and able to work collaboratively, openly, and respectfully with one another.

People in XYZ seem unwilling or unable to work collaboratively, openly, or respectfully with one another.

11. External Communications

1	2	3	4	5	6	7	8	9	10	NA _____

XYZ's communications to us are random and provide confused or inconsistent messages.

XYZ's communications to us are carefully targeted and provide clear and consistent messages.

12. Priorities

1	2	3	4	5	6	7	8	9	10	NA _____

XYZ clearly defines its priorities to us.

XYZ does not clearly define its priorities to us.

13. Delegation of Authority

1	2	3	4	5	6	7	8	9	10	NA _____

Decision making and control seem delegated to the lowest appropriate levels in XYZ.

Decision making and control seem retained at inappropriately high levels in XYZ.

14. Recognition

   1   2   3   4   5   6   7   8   9   10   NA _____

   XYZ acknowledges   XYZ does not
   actions that support   acknowledge actions
   its strategies and goals.   that support its strategies
                                             and goals.

15. Creativity

   1   2   3   4   5   6   7   8   9   10   NA _____

   Individuals in XYZ seem   Individuals in XYZ seem
   to be encouraged to   to be discouraged from
   develop new ideas and   developing new ideas or
   to improve operational   from improving operational
   efficiency and effectiveness.   efficiency and effectiveness.

16. Risk Taking

   1   2   3   4   5   6   7   8   9   10   NA _____

   XYZ managers   XYZ managers encourage
   discourage risk   risk taking in support of
   taking in support of   the organization's mission
   the organization's   and strategies.
   mission and strategies.

17. Cross-Departmental or Cross-Functional Work

   1   2   3   4   5   6   7   8   9   10   NA _____

   Individuals are   Individuals are not
   encouraged to work   encouraged to work
   across departmental   across departmental
   and functional lines   and functional lines.
   to achieve their goals.

18. Roles and Responsibilities

   1   2   3   4   5   6   7   8   9   10   NA _____

   Roles and responsibilities   Roles and responsibilities
   are clear and appropriate   are ambiguous in XYZ.
   within XYZ.

19. XYZ Teamwork

    1   2   3   4   5   6   7   8   9   10   NA _____

    Members of management   Members of management
    work effectively together   do not work effectively
    as a team in XYZ.   together as a team in XYZ.

20. Accountability

    1   2   3   4   5   6   7   8   9   10   NA _____

    Individuals in XYZ seem   Individuals in XYZ seem
    to be held accountable.   not to be held accountable.

21. Organizational Knowledge

    1   2   3   4   5   6   7   8   9   10   NA _____

    The purpose and   The purpose and function
    function of each work   of each work group in XYZ
    group in XYZ is effectively   is not known and not
    communicated and understood.   understood.

22. Discussion Forums

    1   2   3   4   5   6   7   8   9   10   NA _____

    XYZ provides occasions   XYZ does not provide any
    or settings in which we   occasions or settings in
    can discuss issues of   which we can discuss
    concern to us.   issues of concern to us.

23. Customer Service

    1   2   3   4   5   6   7   8   9   10   NA _____

    XYZ knows its   XYZ does not know its
    customers and is a   customers and is not a
    customer service organization. customer service
                                    organization.

24. Culture

    1   2   3   4   5   6   7   8   9   10   NA _____

    XYZ's culture fosters a   XYZ's culture diverts it
    commitment to its   from its mission and the
    mission and the satisfaction   satisfaction of its key
    of its key stakeholders.   stakeholders.

III. OPEN QUESTIONS

A. What would you identify as XYZ's most important *strengths?*

1.

2.

3.

4.

5.

B. What would you identify as XYZ's most important *weaknesses?*

1.

2.

3.

4.

5.

C. If you could change anything about the XYZ Organization, what would it be?

    1.

    2.

    3.

    4.

    5.

F. Model Internal Stakeholder Evaluation Questionnaire for XYZ Organization

This questionnaire, for the fictitious XYZ Organization, is presented as a model only. A questionnaire of this type must be tailored to fit the organization in which it is to be administered. Every organization must choose its own best approach when conducting an internal assessment.

CONFIDENTIAL MATERIAL

Date:

To: All Staff

From: General Manager [or "Director" or "Process Champion," and so forth]

First, I would like to thank all of you in advance for taking the time and effort to review and complete the attached questionnaire.

This questionnaire is an opportunity for you to provide feedback on XYZ. It is also your chance to raise stakeholder or customer service improvement issues and suggestions. All ideas will be considered, and the information will be shared with staff at a Town Hall Meeting to be held [date] in the auditorium.

ABC Company (our external consultant) will keep all questionnaires confidential, and the results will be compiled in a manner that does not disclose individual responses.

If possible, please complete the questionnaire electronically as this will speed the process of tabulating the information. Please e-mail the completed questionnaire, as an attachment, to the ABC Company, at [e-mail address].

Your completed questionnaires can also be dropped into the sealed collection boxes provided in the lobby. The ABC Company will pick up the collection boxes. You may also mail your response directly to the ABC Company at [mailing address].

Please return your responses by [date].
Thank you again for your participation.

INTERNAL EVALUATION QUESTIONNAIRE

Please complete the following information:

My XYZ Department is: _____

My Job Group is: _____ Manager/Supervisor (including Technical Services)

_____ Profession/Technician/Craft/Trade (including custodians, vehicle maintenance workers)

_____ Office Support (including clerical, IS, messengers)

Instructions for Completion

There are no "right" or "wrong" answers.

1. For each question in this questionnaire please circle the number from 1 to 10 that most closely reflects how you feel about the set of statements in that question.

2. If a set of statements does not apply to your position in the XYZ Organization, please mark the NA (not applicable) blank.

Please be candid in your responses and draw on your most recent experiences in the last two years.

Sample Question

Resources

| 1 | 2 | 3 | 4 | 5 | 6 | 7 | ⑧ | 9 | 10 | NA _____ |

Resources are likely to increase in the next five years.

Resources are not likely to increase in the next five years.

Circling 1 would indicate a strong agreement with the left-hand statement ("Resources are likely to increase in the next five years").

Circling 10 would indicate strong agreement with the right-hand statement ("Resources are not likely to increase in the next five years").

Circling 8 would indicate moderate agreement with the right-hand statement, and so forth.

If you have any questions please contact Dr. Jane Smith of The ABC Company at [phone number or e-mail address].

I. MISSION, VISION, AND THE ORGANIZATION'S ENVIRONMENT

Successful organizations possess a clear understanding of their situations. They also have established an organizational mission and vision and have communicated it to their employees and stakeholders.

- *Vision* is an image of an organization's desired future state. XYZ's vision is to achieve the greatest value for its stakeholders [or "customers"] through innovative, proactive, and convenient service solutions.

- *Mission* is an organization's overriding purpose. Mission provides a reason for stakeholders to support the organization. The mission of XYZ is to provide services that are high quality, on time, fiscally responsible, and convenient for our stakeholders [or "customers"].

- *Environment* describes the *context* in which XYZ pursues its mission and vision. The *external* environment can present opportunities or challenges (threats), and the *internal* environment can provide strengths on which we can draw and weaknesses we must overcome or minimize.

- *Stakeholders* refers to both internal and external people, groups, and organizations that affect XYZ and are in turn affected by it. All XYZ's employees, unions, and clients, and also the legislature, certain special interest groups, and the media are stakeholders. [Other stakeholders might be "other agencies," "the regulated industry," "consumers," and so on.]

- *Environmental scanning* is the tracking and analysis of factors and trends that do or could affect XYZ, that is, marketplace and business trends, resource use, technological change, new regulations and legislative changes, and so forth.

Questions

1. Relevance of Mission and Vision Statements

1	2	3	4	5	6	7	8	9	10	NA _____

   XYZ's mission and vision
   statements are relevant;
   they accurately reflect
   organizational aspirations
   and environmental realities.

   XYZ's mission and vision
   statements are outdated;
   they no longer reflect
   organizational aspirations
   and environmental realities.

2. Effectiveness of Mission and Vision

1	2	3	4	5	6	7	8	9	10	NA _____

   Individuals and units work
   together in support of a
   common XYZ mission
   and vision.

   Individuals and units work
   toward fulfilling diverse
   missions and visions.

3. Service Versus Procedural Compliance

| 1 | 2 | 3 | 4 | 5 | 6 | 7 | 8 | 9 | 10 | NA _____ |

In our daily activities we are guided by XYZ's mission and vision.

In our daily activities we are oriented toward day-to-day compliance with XYZ's policies and procedures.

4. Knowledge of Stakeholders

| 1 | 2 | 3 | 4 | 5 | 6 | 7 | 8 | 9 | 10 | NA _____ |

We understand our current and potential stakeholders.

We do not have a clear understanding of our current or potential stakeholders.

5. Environmental Scanning

| 1 | 2 | 3 | 4 | 5 | 6 | 7 | 8 | 9 | 10 | NA _____ |

We routinely monitor changes in our work environment that could affect XYZ, and we assess potential losses or reductions in services and potential opportunities.

We do not routinely monitor changes in our work environment that might affect XYZ.

6. Response to the Environment

| 1 | 2 | 3 | 4 | 5 | 6 | 7 | 8 | 9 | 10 | NA _____ |

XYZ works to define its future within the context of changing factors in the environment; it responds proactively to its environment.

XYZ addresses changing factors in the environment only when they begin to be felt; it responds reactively to its environment.

7. Attitude Toward Change

| 1 | 2 | 3 | 4 | 5 | 6 | 7 | 8 | 9 | 10 | NA _____ |

Overall, XYZ responds to change by seeing opportunities.

Overall, XYZ tends to avoid change or to view it as high risk.

Comments

Please use the following space to comment on XYZ's mission and vision.

You may include items not specifically addressed in the questionnaire questions or expand on your responses to particular questionnaire items.

If you prefer, you may write out your comments in a separate file, titled "Comments I," or on separate pieces of paper. Be sure to attach this separate file to your e-mail or mail the papers with the questionnaire when it is returned.

II. BUDGET, HUMAN RESOURCES, AND INFORMATION TECHNOLOGY

This section of the questionnaire focuses on the management of budgets, human resources, and information technology. Successful organizations and managers achieve their mission and attain their vision by effectively managing their resources.

Questions

8. Internal Budgeting Process

1	2	3	4	5	6	7	8	9	10	NA _____

XYZ's budgeting process is clearly defined and communicated and consistently followed.

XYZ's budgeting process is not clearly defined or communicated or consistently followed.

9. Allocation of Staff and Funds

1	2	3	4	5	6	7	8	9	10	NA _____

Our staff and dollars are clearly linked to XYZ's mission and priorities.

Our staff and dollars are not linked to XYZ's mission and priorities.

10. Information Technology

1	2	3	4	5	6	7	8	9	10	NA _____

We use technology effectively in managing XYZ's resources and pursuing its mission.

We make ineffective use of information technology in managing XYZ's resources and pursuing its mission.

11. Management Respect

1	2	3	4	5	6	7	8	9	10	NA _____

I generally feel that management respects me as a person and values the work I do.

I generally feel that management does not respect me enough or value the work I do.

12. Supervisor Respect

1	2	3	4	5	6	7	8	9	10	NA _____

I generally feel that my supervisor respects me as a person and values the work I do.

I generally feel that my supervisor does not respect me enough or value the work I do.

13. Performance Measures

1	2	3	4	5	6	7	8	9	10	NA ____

Clear performance measures exist that link my work to XYZ's mission and goals.

Clear performance measures that link my work to XYZ's mission and goals do not exist.

14. Job Satisfaction

1	2	3	4	5	6	7	8	9	10	NA ____

In general I am not satisfied with my job.

In general I am satisfied with my job.

15. Advancement

1	2	3	4	5	6	7	8	9	10	NA ____

There is a lack of opportunities for advancement within XYZ.

There are adequate opportunities for advancement within XYZ.

16. Empowerment

1	2	3	4	5	6	7	8	9	10	NA ____

I feel empowered to work effectively and efficiently in XYZ.

I do not feel empowered to work effectively and efficiently in XYZ.

17. Compensation

1	2	3	4	5	6	7	8	9	10	NA ____

My level of compensation is appropriate for my work.

My level of compensation is not appropriate for my work.

Comments

Please use the following space to comment on any of XYZ's significant strengths or weaknesses in the areas of budgets, human resources, and information technology.

You may address issues not specifically raised in the questionnaire questions or expand on your responses to particular questionnaire items.

If you prefer, you may write out your comments in a separate file, titled "Comments II," or on separate pieces of paper. Be sure to attach this separate file to your e-mail or mail the papers with the questionnaire when it is returned.

III. COMMUNICATIONS

This section examines the flow of information within XYZ. Successful organizations transmit clear messages, have well-developed communication networks, and have adequate forums to promote discussion and dialogue.

- *Messages* are clear, concise, and targeted toward specific stakeholders and designed to produce specific responses.

- *Communication networks* effectively convey information to both internal and external stakeholders.

- *Forums* provide the occasions and settings for appropriate discussion and dialogue.

Questions

18. Definition of Decision-Making Processes

1	2	3	4	5	6	7	8	9	10	NA _____

XYZ's decision-making processes are poorly defined.

XYZ's decision-making processes are clearly defined.

19. Adherence to Decision-Making Processes

1	2	3	4	5	6	7	8	9	10	NA _____

Decision-making processes are inconsistently followed in XYZ.

Decision-making processes are consistently followed in XYZ.

20. Information

1	2	3	4	5	6	7	8	9	10	NA _____

In XYZ, information is viewed as a resource and is generally shared.

In XYZ, information is used as a basis for power and is generally tightly controlled.

21. Synergy

1	2	3	4	5	6	7	8	9	10	NA _____

In general, people in XYZ are willing and able to work collaboratively, openly, and respectfully with one another.

In general, people in XYZ are unwilling or unable to work collaboratively, openly, or respectfully with one another.

22. Black Holes

| 1 | 2 | 3 | 4 | 5 | 6 | 7 | 8 | 9 | 10 | NA _____ |

XYZ has some organizational black holes where information becomes distorted, inconsistent, or stalled.

Information is communicated throughout XYZ in a clear, consistent, and timely manner.

23. Information Technology

| 1 | 2 | 3 | 4 | 5 | 6 | 7 | 8 | 9 | 10 | NA _____ |

XYZ uses technology effectively to facilitate and enhance communications, both internally and externally.

XYZ does not use technology effectively to facilitate or enhance internal or external communications.

24. External Communications

| 1 | 2 | 3 | 4 | 5 | 6 | 7 | 8 | 9 | 10 | NA _____ |

XYZ's communications to its customers are random and provide confused or inconsistent messages.

XYZ's communications to its customers are carefully targeted and provide clear and consistent messages.

25. Discussion Forums

| 1 | 2 | 3 | 4 | 5 | 6 | 7 | 8 | 9 | 10 | NA _____ |

XYZ provides forums in which we can discuss issues of concern to us.

XYZ does not provide any occasions or settings in which we can discuss issues of concern to us.

Comments

Please use the following space to comment on any significant XYZ strengths or weaknesses in the area of communications.

You may address issues not specifically raised in the questionnaire questions or expand on your responses to particular questionnaire items.

If you prefer, you may write out your comments in a separate file, titled "Comments III," or on separate pieces of paper. Be sure to attach this separate file to your e-mail or mail the papers with the questionnaire when it is returned.

IV. LEADERSHIP, MANAGEMENT, STRUCTURE, PROCESSES, AND CULTURE

This section examines various aspects of leadership, management, and organizational structures and processes.

Successful organizations enjoy inspirational leadership, competent management, and organize themselves in strategic ways.

- *Leadership* may be defined as making sure that XYZ is doing the right things.

- *Management* may be defined as making sure that those right things are being done right.

- *Structures and processes* embody the purposeful organizing of relationships and flows across and up and down XYZ in order to carry out specific strategic initiatives.

Questions

26. Senior Administrative Leadership (XYZ Deputy Director and above)

1	2	3	4	5	6	7	8	9	10	NA _____

The senior administrators spend sufficient time on leadership activities.

The senior administrators spend too little time providing leadership.

27. Midlevel Management

1	2	3	4	5	6	7	8	9	10	NA _____

Midlevel administrators spend sufficient time on management activities.

Midlevel administrators spend too little time on management activities.

28. Priorities

1	2	3	4	5	6	7	8	9	10	NA _____

XYZ clearly defines its priorities.

XYZ does not clearly define its priorities.

29. Delegation of Authority

1	2	3	4	5	6	7	8	9	10	NA _____

Decision making and control in XYZ are delegated to the lowest appropriate levels.

Decision making and control in XYZ are retained at inappropriately high levels.

30. Recognition

| 1 | 2 | 3 | 4 | 5 | 6 | 7 | 8 | 9 | 10 | NA _____ |

XYZ consistently acknowledges actions that support its strategies and goals.

XYZ does not consistently acknowledge actions that support its strategies and goals.

31. Professional Development

| 1 | 2 | 3 | 4 | 5 | 6 | 7 | 8 | 9 | 10 | NA _____ |

Professional development opportunities are limited in XYZ, or individuals are frequently constrained from taking advantage of them.

XYZ is committed to professional development at all levels.

32. Creativity

| 1 | 2 | 3 | 4 | 5 | 6 | 7 | 8 | 9 | 10 | NA _____ |

Individuals are encouraged to develop new ideas and to improve operational efficiency and effectiveness.

Individuals are discouraged from developing new ideas, or from improving operational efficiency and effectiveness.

33. Risk Taking

| 1 | 2 | 3 | 4 | 5 | 6 | 7 | 8 | 9 | 10 | NA _____ |

Managers discourage risk taking in support of the organizational mission and strategies.

Managers encourage risk taking in support of the organizational mission and strategies.

34. Cross-Departmental or Cross-Functional Work

| 1 | 2 | 3 | 4 | 5 | 6 | 7 | 8 | 9 | 10 | NA _____ |

Individuals are encouraged to work across departmental and functional lines to achieve their goals.

Individuals are not encouraged to work across departmental and functional lines.

35. Technology

| 1 | 2 | 3 | 4 | 5 | 6 | 7 | 8 | 9 | 10 | NA _____ |

XYZ effectively and proactively applies technology to improve management and operational effectiveness.

XYZ's use of technology for management or operational purposes is haphazard to nonexistent.

36. Functions and Activities

| 1 | 2 | 3 | 4 | 5 | 6 | 7 | 8 | 9 | 10 | NA _____ |

Some necessary functions and activities are not properly planned or are missing, duplicated, or not clearly assigned.

All necessary functions and activities are properly planned, clearly assigned, and routinely fulfilled.

37. Roles and Responsibilities

| 1 | 2 | 3 | 4 | 5 | 6 | 7 | 8 | 9 | 10 | NA _____ |

Roles and responsibilities are clear and appropriate.

Roles and responsibilities are ambiguous or inappropriate.

38. Administrative Support

| 1 | 2 | 3 | 4 | 5 | 6 | 7 | 8 | 9 | 10 | NA _____ |

The administrative and secretarial support is adequate.

The administrative and secretarial support is not adequate.

39. Work Assignments

| 1 | 2 | 3 | 4 | 5 | 6 | 7 | 8 | 9 | 10 | NA _____ |

I generally receive clear and complete instructions when work is assigned.

I generally do not receive clear and complete instructions when work is assigned.

40. Teamwork

| 1 | 2 | 3 | 4 | 5 | 6 | 7 | 8 | 9 | 10 | NA _____ |

Members of management in XYZ work effectively together as a team.

Members of management in XYZ do not work effectively together as a team.

41. Work Priorities

1	2	3	4	5	6	7	8	9	10	NA _____

    XYZ has set clear and understandable work priorities that are adhered to.

    XYZ has not set clear and understandable work priorities that are adhered to.

42. Accountability

1	2	3	4	5	6	7	8	9	10	NA _____

    Individuals are held accountable for use of resources and completing assigned tasks.

    Individuals are not held accountable for the use of resources and assigned tasks.

43. Program-Related Knowledge

1	2	3	4	5	6	7	8	9	10	NA _____

    Individuals are well informed about policies, regulations, and industry standards.

    Individuals have insufficient knowledge about policies, regulations, and industry standards.

44. System Knowledge

1	2	3	4	5	6	7	8	9	10	NA _____

    Individuals know how their assignment areas affect the work of others and fit into XYZ systems and processes.

    Individuals do not know how their own work affects that of others and fits into XYZ systems and processes.

45. Organizational Knowledge

1	2	3	4	5	6	7	8	9	10	NA _____

    The purpose and function of work groups in XYZ is effectively communicated and understood.

    The purpose and function of each work group in XYZ is not known and not understood.

46. Customer Service

1	2	3	4	5	6	7	8	9	10	NA _____

    We know our customers and XYZ is a customer service organization.

    We do not know our customers and XYZ is not a customer service organization.

Comments

Please use the following space to comment on any significant strengths or weaknesses in the areas of leadership, management, structure, processes, and culture.

You may address issues not specifically raised in the questionnaire questions, or expand on your responses to particular questionnaire items.

If you prefer, you may write out your comments in a separate file, titled "Comments IV," or on separate pieces of paper. Be sure to attach this separate file to your e-mail or mail the papers with the questionnaire when it is returned.

V. OPEN QUESTIONS

A. What would you identify as XYZ's most important *strengths?*

1.

2.

3.

4.

5.

B. What would you identify as XYZ's most important *weaknesses?*

1.

2.

3.

4.

5.

C. If you could change anything about XYZ, what would it be?

1.

2.

3.

4.

5.

Thank you for your effort in completing this questionnaire.

G. Analyzing and Reporting Results of Surveys

It is important to discuss your organization's internal and external survey results and explore their implications. What do the answers imply in terms of possible strategic or operational issues, concerns, or opportunities? What does the distribution of the answers imply? They are likely to show that your organization does very well with some stakeholders, clients, or customers but not others. Why is that?

Discussion of your organization's results in facilitated sessions with a broad cross-section of stakeholders can produce not only a good list of possible strategic and operational issues but typically many suggestions for strategies and actions as well. Participation in discussing the results of these surveys usually heightens ownership of the issues, the strategic planning process, and the resulting strategic plan.

Do not be afraid to use customized versions of the surveys presented in Resources E and F and to discuss the results with stakeholders. The truth is that organizations and their stakeholders have few secrets. Most people are aware of the real underlying problems, and if these problems are not raised and discussed, the credibility of the strategic planning process is hurt and the real issues go unaddressed.

To assist people in making sense of the results of the surveys, it is important to report the data in ways that are clear and easy to read. We suggest using graphs. Figure 7 illustrates how the XYZ Organization's survey results might be displayed for two questions, one from an external and one from an internal survey.

Figure 7 ■ Examples of Reporting Survey Results

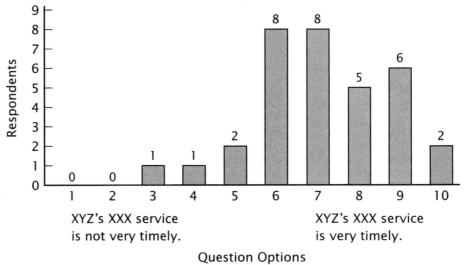

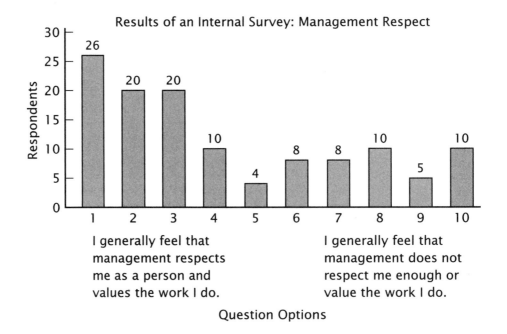

Glossary

Action plan   A plan for the day-to-day operation of a business over the next one to twelve months. It includes a prioritized list of proposed projects as well as plans for all projects that have been funded. Development of an action plan requires no more than two months. The action plan should be reviewed and updated weekly.

Competencies   Capabilities, sets of actions, or strategies at which the organization is particularly good, or the resources (broadly conceived) on which it can draw to perform well on its critical success factors. A **distinctive competency** is a competency that is difficult for others to replicate and so is a source of enduring organizational advantage. A **core competency** is central to the success of the organization. A **distinctive core competency** is central to the success of the organization and hard for others to replicate.

Critical success factors   The things the organization must do, or criteria it must meet, in order to be successful in the eyes of its key stakeholders, especially those in its external environment.

Goal   A long-term organizational target or direction of development. It states what the organization wants to accomplish or become over the next several years. Goals provide a basis for decisions about the nature, scope, and relative priorities of all projects and activities. Everything the organization does should help it move toward attainment of one or more goals.

Mandate   Something the organization is required to do, particularly a requirement imposed by an external actor. Mandates may be formal—laws, rules, regulations—or informal—political mandates for change, for example.

Milestone   A significant date or event during execution of a project, often associated with the end of a phase or subphase.

Mission statement   A statement of organizational purpose.

Objective   A measurable target that must be met on the way to attaining a goal.

Performance measure   A means of objectively assessing the results of programs, products, projects, or services.

Stakeholder   Any person, group, or organization that can place a claim on an organization's attention, resources, or output or that is affected by that output.

Strategic planning   A disciplined effort to produce fundamental decisions and actions that shape and guide what an organization is, what it does, and why it does it.

Strategy   The means by which an organization intends to accomplish a goal or objective. It summarizes a pattern across policy, programs, projects, decisions, and resource allocations.

Values statement   A description of the code of behavior (in relation to employees, other key stakeholders, and society at large) to which an organization adheres or aspires.

Vision sketch   A brief description of what the organization will look like if it succeeds in implementing its strategies and achieves its full potential. A vision sketch is shorter and less detailed than a vision of success.

Vision of success   A description of what an organization will look like if it succeeds in implementing its strategies and achieves its full potential. Often this statement includes the organization's mission, basic philosophy and core values, goals, basic strategies, performance criteria, important decision-making rules, and ethical standards expected of all employees.

Bibliography

Ackermann, F., Eden, C., and Brown, I. *The Practice of Making Strategy.* Thousand Oaks, Calif.: Sage, 2004.

Allison, M., and Kaye, J. *Strategic Planning for Nonprofit Organizations: A Practical Guide and Workbook.* New York: Wiley, 1997.

Barry, B. W. *Strategic Planning Workbook for Nonprofit Organizations.* (2nd ed.) Saint Paul, Minn.: Amherst H. Wilder Foundation, 1997.

Bryson, J. M. *Strategic Planning for Public and Nonprofit Organizations.* (Rev. ed.) San Francisco: Jossey-Bass, 1995.

Bryson, J. M. *Strategic Planning for Public and Nonprofit Organizations.* (3rd ed.) San Francisco: Jossey-Bass, 2004.

Bryson, J. M. "What to Do When Stakeholders Matter: Stakeholder Identification and Analysis Techniques." *Public Management Review,* 2004, *6*(1), 21–53.

Bryson, J. M., Ackermann, F., Eden, C., and Finn, C. B. *Visible Thinking: Unlocking Causal Mapping for Practical Business Results.* New York: Wiley, 2004.

Bryson, J. M., and Anderson, S. R. "Applying Large-Group Interaction Methods in the Planning and Implementation of Major Change Efforts." *Public Administration Review,* 2000, *60*(2), 143–162.

Bryson, J. M., and Crosby, B. C. *Leadership for the Common Good: Tackling Public Problems in a Shared-Power World.* San Francisco: Jossey-Bass, 1992.

Eden, C., and Ackermann, F. *Making Strategy: The Journey of Strategic Management.* Thousand Oaks, Calif.: Sage, 1998.

Holman, P., and Devane, T. E. *The Change Handbook: Group Methods for Shaping the Future.* San Francisco: Berrett-Koehler, 1999.

Johnson, D. W., and Johnson, F. P. *Joining Together: Group Theory and Group Skills.* (7th ed.) Upper Saddle River, N.J.: Prentice Hall, 2002.

Johnson, G., and Scholes, K. *Exploring Corporate Strategy.* (6th ed.) Harlow, England: Pearson Education, 2002.

Mintzberg, H., Ahlstrand, B., and Lampel, J. *Strategy Safari: A Guided Tour Through the Wilds of Strategic Management.* New York: Free Press, 1998.

Mintzberg, H., and Westley, F. "Cycles of Organizational Change." *Strategic Management Journal,* 1992, *13,* 39–59.

Nutt, P. C. *Why Decisions Fail.* San Francisco: Berrett-Koehler, 2002.

Nutt, P. C., and Backoff, R. W. *Strategic Management of Public and Third Sector Organizations: A Handbook for Leaders.* San Francisco: Jossey-Bass, 1992.

Schwarz, R. M. *The Skilled Facilitator: Practical Wisdom for Developing Effective Groups.* (Rev. ed.) San Francisco: Jossey-Bass, 2002.

Spencer, L. *Winning Through Participation.* Dubuque, Iowa: Kendall/Hunt, 1989.

Thomas, J. C. *Public Participation in Public Decisions.* San Francisco: Jossey-Bass, 1995.